HARMONY

FOR EAR, EYE, AND KEYBOARD

(*FIRST YEAR*)

BY

ARTHUR EDWARD HEACOX, MUS. B.

PROFESSOR OF THEORY, OBERLIN CONSERVATORY
OF MUSIC, OBERLIN COLLEGE

AUTHOR OF *Choral Studies, Ear-Training
Elementary Harmony, Lessons in Harmony (Parts I and II)
Keyboard-Training in Harmony*

EAR-TRAINING OUTLINE IN EACH LESSON

By GLADYS FERRY MOORE, MUS. B.

ASSISTANT PROFESSOR OF HARMONY AND EAR-TRAINING
OBERLIN CONSERVATORY OF MUSIC

$1.50

OLIVER DITSON COMPANY
THEODORE PRESSER CO., DISTRIBUTORS
1712 CHESTNUT STREET, PHILADELPHIA
MADE IN U. S. A.

Copyright, MCMXXII and MCMXXIII
By Oliver Ditson Company

International Copyright Secured

TO
THE HUNDREDS OF STUDENTS WHOSE FRIENDLY CO-OPERATION HAS EVER BEEN THE UNFAILING INSPIRATION OF THE AUTHOR'S CLASS-ROOM AND HAS IN LARGE MEASURE HELPED TO MAKE THIS BOOK POSSIBLE.

Harmony Contents

Lesson		Page
1	Study of Harmony like Language Study. Definitions.	1
2	Major Scales, Chord, Triad, Position, Harmonizing a Melody	5
3	To Find the Keys in Sharps, Selection of Triads	9
4	Close and Open Position	12
5	The Five Rules	15
6	Interchange of Close and Open Position, Notation	19
7	Notation (Con.)	22
8	To Find the Keys in Flats, Chord Repetition	24
9	Harmonizing 1-2 of the Scale	27
10	Intervals, To Read Intervals, Inversion of, Minor Intervals	29
11	Special Names of Members of the Key, Minor Triads in minor	32
12	Minor Scales, Original and Harmonic Forms, Relative Keys	35
13	Harmonizing minor melodies	39
14	Cadences, The Period;	41
15	Review	43
16	Figured Bass, Origin, Present Value, Source, The Figures, Inversion of Triads	46
17	The Six-four Chord, Position in Cadence	50
18	The Chord of the Sixth	52
19	The Six-four Chord and the Chord of the Sixth continued	55
20	Passing Tones, Kinds of Motion, Third doubled or omitted	58
21	Accented Passing Tones, Embellishment	61
22	Some Other Six-four Chords, Embellishing, Passing, etc.	63
23	Broken Chord Version of a Period, Accompaniment to Violin	66
24	Review	69
25	Diminished and Augmented Intervals, Table of Intervals	71
26	The Dominant Seventh Chord, Rules for Resolution, Importance to the Composer, Introduction of the Seventh	74
27	Inversions of the Dominant Seventh Chord, Resolutions	78
28	All the Triads, Triad Table in Major	81
29	All the Triads (concluded) Table in Minor, Complete Table	84
30	The Secondary Triads in Major, Rule for II-V, Covered Octaves and Covered Fifths	86
31	Secondary Triads in Major (continued), Rule for II-I$_4^6$, the Deceptive Cadence	90
32	Secondary Triads in Minor, Augmented Second, Overlapping	93
33	The Triad on the Leading Tone, Consecutive Chords of the Sixth	96
34	Rules and Exceptions, Similar Motion of All Four Voices, Leading Tone not Doubled	99
35	The Supertonic Seventh Chord, Cadencing Resolution, Strict Usage in First Lessons, Rules for	102
36	The Sequence, Design Justifies Licenses	105
37	Review	108
38	Modulation by the Dominant Seventh Chord, Defining the New Key, Cadence to Establish the New Key	110
39	Approach New Leading Tone from above, Modulation con.	114
40	From a Major or Minor Key to its Relative ;	117
41	Common Chord Modulation, Keys Overlap	120
42	Common Chord Modulation concluded	123
43	Bach's Figured Chorals, the Schemelli Gesangbuch	125
44	Construction of a Hymn Tune, Importance of the Choice of Cadences;	128
45	Original Work, Three Types Compared	131
46	Next Related Keys, Completing the Modulations by V^7 to	134
47	Review	137
48	The Suspension	140
49	Harmonizing a Folk-Song as a Piece for the Piano	143
50	The Appoggiatura, Broken Chord Accompaniment	146
51	Construction of a Small Primary Form, Cadence Symbols	149
52	Choosing Rhythms, Original Work	152
53	Ornamental Resolution, Violin with Piano Accompaniment	155
54	Review	158
55	The Dominant Ninth Chord, The Ninth as a Suspension or Appoggiatura	160
56	The Remaining Chords of the Seventh	163
57	The Supertonic Seventh Chord Chromatically Altered, Construction of a Little Prelude	166
58	Transient Modulation, Modulating Sequences . ;	169
59	Pianoforte Style Chiefly Homophonic, Freedom of	172
60	Conclusion, Soldiers' Chorus, original March	174
	Appendix A, Reference List	176
	Appendix B, Examination Papers	179

Ear-Training Contents

Lesson		Page
2	Harmonic—primary triads	7
3	Chord-position. Tonal—scale progressions and leaps found between tones of the tonic chord	10
4	Tonal-groups. Review of	13
5	Sight-singing—vocalises. Review ear-training	17
6	Notation. Verbal dictation—quarter-note notation—treble staff	20
7	Notation. Verbal dictation—half-note and eighth-note notation—bass staff—two parts. Sight-singing	23
8	Part-singing—folk-songs. Review of chord position	25
9	Melodic—very simple melodies. Review of primary triads and chord position	27
10	Vocalises. Tonal groups—leap of a third. Intervals—major and minor thirds, seconds, sevenths. Comparison of major and minor triads	30
11	Character of scale-tones. Sight-singing	33
12	Major and minor triads. Major and minor sixths. Verbal dictation—speed work	37
13	Melodic—hints on memorizing. Part-singing—folk-songs. Interval drill	39
14	Sight-singing. Review of triad position and color. Intervals. Harmonic—cadences	42
15	Review	43
16	Key and interval drill. Tonal groups—leaps to tendency tones. Harmonic—triad inversion	48
17	Harmonic—primary triads and their inversions—cadences. First written exercises (soprano and bass)—root position only	50
18	Sight-singing—observation of melodic structure. Harmonic—inversions in written exercises	53
19	Key and interval drill. Melodic—rests—sequence	55
20	Tonal groups, intervals, melodies, in review. Aural harmonization of melodies including passing tones	59
21	Melodic—passing tones, embellishments. Harmonic—review	61
22	The dotted quarter and eighth in *America*. Rhythmic tapping. Harmonic—review. Verbal dictation—two parts	64
23	Chromatic scale	67
24	Review	69
25	Key and interval drill—chromatics. Melodic—two parts—augmented and diminished intervals	73

Lesson		Page
26	Sight-reading — two parts. Melodic—two parts—chromatics. Harmonic—V^7	76
27	Melodic—more difficult melodies. Harmonic—inversions of V^7	79
28	Melodic—original answers to given phrases. Review of chromatic scale	82
29	Review	85
30	Minor mode. Tonal groups in minor	87
31	Varied drill in minor—easy minor melodies	91
32	Sight-singing—minor. Melodic — singing answers in minor. Harmonic—deceptive cadence	94
33	Harmonic—written—minor	97
34	Part-singing—folk-songs. Tonal groups—chromatics	101
35	Melodic—6-8 measure—Chromatics	103
36	Melodic—original work—sequence—ornaments	106
37	Review	108
38	Part-singing—folk-songs. Melodic—bass staff	112
39	Melodic—Harmonic—review, and III6 in cadence	115
40	Key and interval drill in minor. Verbal dictation—minor. Melodic—two parts	118
41	Sight-singing—and its various combinations. Melodic—	121
42	Harmonic—review in major and minor	123
43	Part-singing—folk-songs. Melodic—minor	125
44	Sight-singing — Melodic—	129
45	Melodic—two parts. Harmonic—VI and II	132
46	Sight-singing. Harmonic—comparison of IV and ii^6	136
47	Review	137
48	Chord color—|¡|°|' V^7 Harmonic—IV and II^6	141
49	Chord color. Melodic—more difficult melodies in review	144
50	Sight-singing. Harmonic—II^6	147
51	Melodic—original work	150
52	Harmonic—three and four-chord review problems	153
53	Chord color. Harmonic—the scale harmonized—short review problems	156
54	Review	158
55	Sight-singing. Harmonic—modulation to closely related keys	161
56	Harmonic—modulation continued. General review from this point on, selected by the teacher	164

PREFACE

The aim of this little book is to provide, in lesson form, attractive material for the first year of harmony study in high school or college. The principal features of the plan are as follows:

> 1. Provision is made in each lesson for a threefold approach to the subject; that is, approach through the ear, through the eye, and through the hand. In other words, ear-training and keyboard-training *lead to the written work* and are co-ordinate with it.

> 2. Practice is provided in several styles of original composition, thereby linking up the student's harmony course with his practical music.

> 3. A substantial beginning is established in pure part-writing from both melody and figured bass, with the purpose of laying the foundation necessary for intelligent advanced study.

The plan is not a new one. On the contrary, it is based upon standard authorities, supplemented by observation of what many of our foremost educators in this field are doing at the present day.

Grateful acknowledgment is here made of the generous assistance and friendly counsel of Dr. Charles Hubert Farnsworth, Associate Professor of School of Music, Teachers College, Columbia University; Mr. Glenn H. Woods, A. A. G. O., Director of Music, Oakland City Schools, Oakland, California; and of Miss Lucy M. Haywood, Head of the Department of Harmony and Music History in the high schools of Lincoln, Nebraska. I am also genuinely appreciative of the co-operation of my colleagues at Oberlin College: Karl Wilson Gehrkens, A. M., Professor of School Music; Dr. George Whitfield Andrews, Professor of Organ and Composition; Friedrich Johann Lehmann, Professor of Theory; Mrs. Bertha McCord Miller, Principal of the Children's Department and Assistant Professor of the Normal Course in Piano;

Miss Florence Livingston Joy, A. M., Instructor in English; and, finally, of Miss Gladys Ferry Moore, Mus. B., Assistant Professor of Harmony and Ear-Training, who, from the laboratory of her own class-room, has provided the indispensable ear-training outlines which form a part of each lesson.

Arthur E. Heacox

Oberlin, Ohio.
July, 1922.

TO THE TEACHER

The Book The book can be completed in 120 60-minute recitation periods or in 150 45-minute periods, with approximately an equal amount of outside preparation. This makes a one-year course for the high school class which meets five times per week and allows ample time for review lessons and examinations. If taken as a one-year course it is recommended that the second semester begin with the subject of *Modulation* (Lesson 38).

In many schools it may be desirable to extend the work over a longer period of time with but two or three class sessions per week. If taken as a two year course, begin the second semester with *Passing Tones* (Lesson 20), the third semester with *Modulation* (Lesson 38), and the fourth semester with *Harmonizing a Folk-Song* (Lesson 49). Suggested examinations for the end of each of these divisions will be found in Appendix B.

A. E. H.

Ear-Training and Sight-Singing For the ear-training and sight-singing course, teachers who use this book should always supplement the text material with material from other sources. To give, here, the requisite amount of working material is impossible: the size of the book prohibits; the emphasis to be placed on any one point varies with the individual student; obviously, much material should be new to the learner. That the teacher may have wide supplementary resources, he should aim to own many of the text-books named in Appendix A, I to V inclusive. If creative, he can invent exercises. He should not change the key frequently — probably it is best to use only one key in each lesson — and he should increase the difficulty of the exercises as fast as the class gains assurance and speed.

The choice of sight-singing material is left to the teacher. It should be planned in such a way that it will correlate with the ear-training, each new problem being sung before it is written.

The ear-training course may be considered flexible, the outline merely giving helpful suggestions along the way. The ear should be appealed to with the entrance of each new subject; that is, throughout the course there should be some correlation between the harmony and the ear-training. But there should always be sufficient review drill on each point to enable the students to master that point before going on to a new one. The amount of time to be spent on any one problem can not be determined outside of the classroom itself.

The use of *two minute* drill periods on review problems is strongly urged. The teacher will be surprised at the amount which can be accomplished in this way, and it will enable him to do several kinds of things within the allotted fifteen or twenty minutes.

The best results in the melodic work will be attained by the use of the syllables. For all interval, triad, and harmonic drill use a neutral syallable, *la*, unless the syllables are specifically mentioned in the text.

Although no rhythm is indicated in the tonal exercises, it is best to play them rhythmically. For instance: —

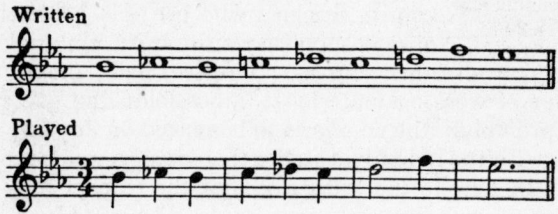

Good material in minor seems somewhat scarce, but do not neglect the minor mode because of this fact. Get the students to invent their own minor melodies. For training them to think in minor, there is nothing better than original work under a guiding hand.

G. F. M.

HARMONY
FOR EAR, EYE, AND KEYBOARD

HARMONY

For Ear, Eye, and Keyboard

(FIRST YEAR)

LESSON 1

Study of Harmony like Language Study

The study of *Harmony* is much like the study of a language. In fact, the parallel is strikingly close. In a language one must learn in detail the letters; how they appear to the eye, how they sound to the ear, and how to write and to pronounce them. Just so, the scales are the A, B, C of harmony; and one must know how they are constructed, how they sound, and how to write them, sing them, and play them.

In a language one learns to spell words and construct sentences. So in harmony, from the musical scale one builds intervals and chords, and from these builds the phrases which form the basis of practically all harmonic writing.

Then again, in a language one studies the masterpieces of the great classic writers and thereby acquires an appreciation of and a taste for the purest and noblest forms of thought expression. Furthermore, it is not enough merely to read such things. One need the guiding hand of an inspiring teacher who can reveal the beauty of these masterpieces through analysis of their content and a more minute study of the technic of thought expression. So, in the study of harmony, one may be said to enter the laboratory of the great composer, become acquainted with the medium in which he works, observe how he builds his rhythms, his melodies, his chords; see, eventually, how he combines all these in his phrases and periods, and fashions, at last, complete works of enduring beauty.

Those who bring to this subject a musical ear, a fine enthusiasm for earnest work in this field, and the courage and faithfulness necessary to succeed in any worthy endeavor, may confidently expect to reap a rich reward from their study of this beautiful tone-language, the language of music — Harmony.

Preliminary Definitions[1] *Sound* may be considered under two general divisions: *Tone* and *Noise*. Tone is a sound which has definite pitch; Noise, a sound which has no definite pitch.

A *Tone* is produced by a body (for example, a violin string, a reed, or a column of air) vibrating *regularly* more than sixteen times in a second. Middle C on the piano is produced by 261 vibrations per second. This is International Pitch. Band instruments are often made at a so-called concert pitch, which makes Middle C nearly a halfstep higher than International.

A *Note* is a character which expresses relative duration. When placed on a staff it indicates that a certain tone is to be sounded for a certain relative length of time.

The *Staff* consists of a number of parallel lines, usually five, with the spaces belonging to them. Each line or space is called a *degree*.

A *Clef* is a character which causes the degree of the staff with which it is associated to indicate a definite pitch. By inference the pitch of the other lines and spaces is shown.

The *G clef* locates the first G above Middle C on the second line of the staff; the *F clef*, the first F below Middle C on the fourth line. The *C clef*, used in ancient vocal scores and for some orchestral instruments, locates Middle C on any degree on which it is placed. These clefs are in fact corruptions of the letters G, F, and C which were formerly used just as we now use the clefs.

The *Signature* is the sign of the key; i. e., the sharps or flats (or their absence) at the beginning of the staff.

A *Key* is a family of tones bearing a definite and close relation to one principal tone called the keynote (key-tone).

---

[1] For study, or for reference only, at the discretion of the teacher. Much will depend upon the previous preparation of the pupils.

The *Keynote* is that tone of a key from which all the others are determined and which makes the best point of closing.

A *Half-step* is the distance from any tone to the next available tone either above or below; e. g., on the piano, C to B, C to C♯. (In our notation we have no means of indicating distances smaller than the half-step.)

Half-steps are of two kinds; *chromatic* and *diatonic*.

A *Chromatic Half-step* is one whose pitches are indicated on the same degree of the staff; e. g., C–C♯, or C–C♭.

A *Diatonic Half-step* is one whose pitches are indicated on adjacent degrees of the staff; e. g., C–B, or C–D♭.

A *Whole-step* consists of two half-steps. It is indicated on adjacent degrees of the staff; e. g., C–D.

Enharmonic means the same pitch differently notated. For example, the enharmonic equivalent of F♯ is G♭.

A *Sharp* (♯) causes the degree of the staff on which it is placed or with which it is associated, as in a key-signature, to indicate a pitch a half-step higher than the degree would without it.

A *Flat* (♭) causes the degree of the staff on which it is placed or with which it is associated, as in a key-signature, to indicate a pitch a half-step lower than the degree would without it.

A *Double Sharp* (×) indicates elevation a whole-step, and a *Double Flat* (♭♭), depression a whole-step from the unaltered degree, whether or not previously sharped or flatted.

A *Natural* (♮) used on any degree cancels the effect of all sharps or flats that have been used on it.

A *Scale* is an ascending or descending series of tones arranged according to some definite plan. Of the many scale forms that have been used at various times and in different countries, but two have any direct bearing on our present study; viz., the *Diatonic* and the *Chromatic*.

A *Chromatic Scale* progresses always by half-steps and contains thirteen tones in the octave.

A *Diatonic Scale* is one which progresses (generally) by steps and half-steps, always in alphabetical order, with eight tones in the octave.

There are two classes of diatonic scales; viz., *Major* and *Minor*.

A *Consonance* is a combination of tones sounding together which requires no further progression; e. g., C–E.

A *Dissonance* is a combination of tones sounding together which gives a sense of unrest, demanding resolution or progression to a consonance; e. g., B–F.

LESSON 2

Major Scales   In order to build and use chords intelligently we must know the scales from which they are derived. We need first to acquire the ability to think, spell, play, and write readily the *major scales*.

The white keys on the piano, from C to C, represent a typical *Major Scale*. Listen to it and observe its pattern. See how it progresses in *alphabetical order*, and note the exact position of the whole and half-steps (the dash indicates whole-steps, and the slur, half-steps):

1—2—3⌣4—5—6—7⌣8. The chief characteristic of a major scale is the *Major Third* (two whole-steps) from 1 to 3.

Form a major scale by applying this pattern beginning on G; also on D, then on A. Observe the necessity of using certain black keys. Visualize this pattern and trace it on the surface of the keys in any octave.

We may also build a chord on each tone of the scale, using 1—3—5 for the first chord, 2—4—6 for the second, and so on. This may be called playing a scale of chords.

A Chord   A chord is a group of tones (three or more) sounded together and bearing a harmonic relation to each other. The simplest chord is the *Triad* (tri=3).

A Triad   A triad consists of a root (fundamental) with the third and the fifth above it. Play a scale of triads in C, in G, in D, in A. Visualize each of these scale-pictures carefully.

Position   A triad does not lose its identity when its root or its third is at the top. These are simply different positions of the chord. Arrange now a scale of triads in C with the root of each at the top. Do the same with the scales of G, D, and A.

Next play each of these chord scales with the third of

each triad at the top. Do all you can to fix these in your memory through the eye, the ear, and the fingers.

Primary Triads Now return again to the white keys and the scale of triads in C major. Compare the sound of these triads and you will agree that there are three kinds. The chords on I, IV, and V (marked with large numerals) form the most important group. See Ex. 1. These three are called the *Primary Triads*. The ii, iii, and vi belong to a second group, while vii° is different from all the others:—

For many lessons our work with chords will be confined to the use of the primary triads, and when we can use them well we shall have made substantial progress in harmony study.

Harmonizing a Melody Let us see what we can do with the primary triads by putting one of them under each tone in the following melody:—

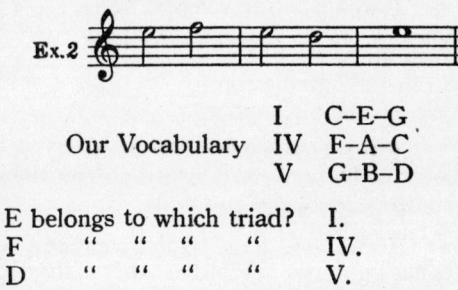

```
                    I    C-E-G
     Our Vocabulary IV   F-A-C
                    V    G-B-D
```

The E belongs to which triad?   I.
 " F   "   "   "   "   IV.
 " D   "   "   "   "   V.

You will then play: I–IV–I–V–I. These will lie in the right hand and are easily reached, for they are within the octave.

What will improve the sound of this? The addition of a bass, or foundation. Like the foundation of a house, the root — or foundation — of each of these chords must be strong. So we will put the root of each triad in the bass also. A chord is in *Root Position* when its root is in the bass. The root now appears both in the bass and in one of the upper parts[1]. This is *doubling the root.* In four-part writing, if the root of these chords is in the bass it is almost always in one other part also.

Now play Ex. 2 harmonized. Sing each part in turn. Play three parts and sing the fourth one. Do this with each part in turn. Can you write it? Two or three may work together at the board in a group if desired. Test each exercise at the piano. Let it be a matter of ear and fingers quite as much as of writing.

EAR-TRAINING

Listen to our completed model and name the chord numbers by ear. When the order of the chords is changed, can you tell the difference between IV and V? (The teacher will play I–V–I–IV–I part of the time.)

ASSIGNMENT

Keyboard Work: Play the major scales of C, G, D, A. Play the scale of triads in each of these four keys, and in each of the three positions, i. e., with the root, third, and fifth in turn at the top.
Harmonize Ex. 2 once more.

Written Work: Write the major scales of C, G, D, A. Harmonize Ex. 2 in four parts and number the chords with the proper Roman numerals.

Oral Recitation: Recite the four scales we have studied, with their signatures. What is the fifth degree in the scale of C? The third in G? The fourth in D, etc.? A is 2 in what scale? D is 6 where, etc.?

---

[1] The illustration of this harmonization, *purposely omitted here*, may be seen, if needed, in Ex. 5 (a).

8   HARMONY FOR EAR, EYE, AND KEYBOARD

Bring your written work copied neatly in ink in a suitable blank book. In these first lessons write the chord for the right hand with one stem, and the bass alone on the bass staff. Place each sharp exactly on its line or in its space. For preliminary practice in pencil you should have a music pad and a good eraser.

In writing the scales follow a model—like the following—where you use the sharp as needed in the scale, and after the scale write the signature and the key letter. A capital letter is used to indicate a major key: —

In writing the signature arrange the sharps in the order of their first appearance, f#, c#, g#. Their particular grouping on the staff has been established by custom as follows:—

ADDITIONAL EXERCISES

(EAR-TRAINING)

Harmonic: (For meaning of 8, 5, 3, see footnote 2, page 43.)

I^8	IV	I	I^8	IV	I	I^5	I^3	V	I
I^5	IV	I	I^5	IV	I	I^8	V	V^5	I
I^3	V	I	I^3	V	I	I^5	IV	IV^5	I
I^5	V	I	I^5	V	V^3	V^5	V^3	I	IV I
I^8	V	I	I^8	V	I	IV	I	V	I
I^3	IV	I	I^3	IV	IV^3	I	I^8	IV	IV^3 I

LESSON 3

Apply the major scale pattern beginning on E, on B, on F♯, and on C♯. Test each scale by the ear as well as by the eye. Observe that the new sharp occurs each time on *seven* of the scale. These successive sharps are a fifth apart; therefore the successive keynotes must be a fifth apart. From this may be derived the following rule:

To Find the Keys In Sharps **The fifth degree of any diatonic scale is the keynote of the following scale in sharps (i. e., with one more sharp).**

As you play each scale, trace the pattern carefully on the keys and acquire a visual memory of it. Spell each scale as you play it. Be sure to use the word *sharp* where needed. Do not say *d, e, f* when you mean *d, e, f*♯.

Play the scale of triads in E, B, F♯, and C♯. Arrange them also as in Lesson 2, with the root at the top, then with the third at the top.

Now play the three *primary triads* of C major, and then those of G, D, A, E, B, F♯, and C♯. See how quickly and accurately you can do this.

Your written work for today contained Ex. 2 harmonized and figured, as in Ex. 5 (*a*):—

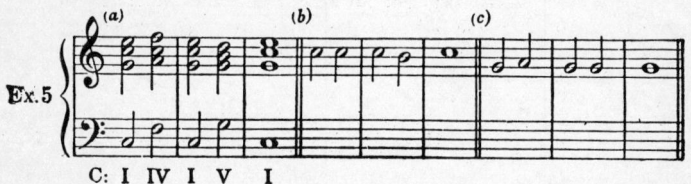

Selection of Triads Let us put primary triads under (*b*). The note C belongs to both I and IV, but the first and last chords would better be I. There is still a chance to choose the triads for the other C's. Try each way. We could play I–I–IV–V–I, or I–I–I–V–I, but the order of triads in (a) is better than either of these.

Experiment in the same way with the last little melody. Here again is a chance to choose. Of course, you have guessed that these are simply three positions of the same chord succession. Listen to each, as played by your teacher, and see how well you can name these chords by ear. (The teacher will sometimes vary the order.)

The term *"diatonic"* means *through the tones*, or from degree to degree in the key. This term refers to all our major and minor scales, as distinguished from the chromatic scale, which always progresses by half-steps.

The following completes the list of sharp signatures. Note that the last signature, reading from left to right, contains all the others: —

EAR-TRAINING

Chord Position: The teacher will play triads (three voices only) and the class will tell whether root, third, or fifth is in the soprano. Compare the distance between the lowest and the middle tones with that between the middle and the upper tones, by singing the intervening scale degrees. Each triad may be considered a tonic triad: —

Melodic: The teacher will play exercises similar to the following model (scale progressions or leaps found between the tones of the tonic triad only), and the class will recite in the following ways:—

1. Sing with the *so—fa* syllables as rapidly as possible.
2. Sing with the letter names.

3. Sing with the number names.
4. Write in whole notes on the music pad.

ASSIGNMENT

Keyboard Work: Play the major scales of E, B, F♯, and C♯. Play the scale of triads in each of these keys. Play Ex. 5 (*a*), (*b*), and (*c*), using the same triad succession each time, as under (*a*). Then transpose each one to G and D.

Written Work: Write the major scales of E, B, F♯, and C♯. Harmonize Ex. 5 (*b*), and (*c*), and write the chord numbers underneath, as before.

Oral Recitation: Drill on all the scales in sharps, as outlined in Lesson 2.

ADDITIONAL EXERCISES

(EAR-TRAINING)

Tonal:—

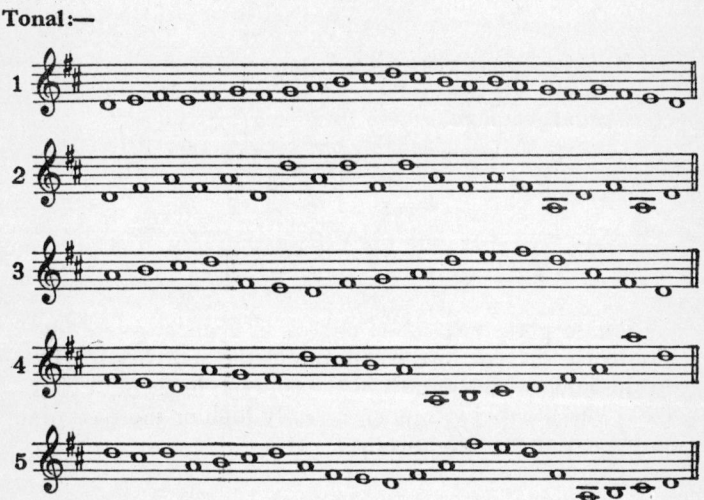

LESSON 4

Close Position   We have seen that the chords in Ex. 5(*a*) can be arranged in three ways over the same bass notes; namely, with the root or the third or the fifth as the soprano in the first triad. In all three ways the right hand could easily play the upper three parts because they lie within an octave of each other.

When the upper three voices (or tones) of a chord lie within an octave, they are said to be in *close position*.

Open Position   Chords do not lose their identity when arranged so as to make the upper three parts extend beyond an octave. When so arranged the chords are said to be in *open position*. In open position keep the alto within an octave of the soprano and tenor.

Let us turn to Ex. 5 (*a*), which is in close position, and spread the chords out into open position. If we call the parts soprano, alto, tenor, and bass, as in a hymn tune, the simplest way to change this to open position will be to play the alto an octave lower (making it a tenor) and leave the other two parts where they are as soprano and alto parts. We then obtain the following:—

Ex. 7

C: I   IV   I   V   I

Try to play these same chords in open position, beginning with the root in the soprano in the first chord. Then do the same with the fifth in the soprano in the first chord. This time the soprano must be fairly high or the bass must be played an octave lower.

Let your teacher play these three positions after you have tried them. Listen intently and compare the sound with the close positions you have already heard. Can you tell the difference? Can you hear the alto, for example, by "focusing" your ear upon it? Or the tenor? If you can do this, your ear is ready for many other interesting things as we reach them from time to time.

EAR-TRAINING

The teacher will sound *do*, the pupils sing it and fix the tone in the memory. Now after *one hearing only*, sing and write groups like the following. Each group is a separate little problem:—

The teacher will play I–IV–V–I in all three positions for the class to name the chord numbers and also the chord position. Also I–I–IV–V–I–IV–I, etc., until, from lesson to lesson, these are named with great readiness.

The teacher will select some book of sight-singing melodies (suggestions will be found in Appendix A), and ask each member of the class to bring a copy next time. Better still, if there are funds for it, buy a set for the school library and loan these to the students.

ASSIGNMENT

Keyboard Work: Play I–V–I in close position (four voices) in all three ways and then the same in open position in three ways; i. e., beginning in turn with the root, third, and fifth in the soprano. In the same way play I–IV–I in all the possible (six) ways.

Written Work: Copy Ex. 7 and arrange it in the other two open positions. Write I–IV–I in four parts in the six ways in F♯.

Note: When you have the tenor on the bass staff, use separate stems for each part, as you see in the model (Ex. 7). Stems up, on the right for the soprano and tenor, and **down,**

14 HARMONY FOR EAR, EYE, AND KEYBOARD

on the left, for the alto and bass. This will help us to think of the parts as real voices moving horizontally instead of merely parts of chords thought vertically.

ADDITIONAL EXERCISES

(EAR-TRAINING)

Tonal:—

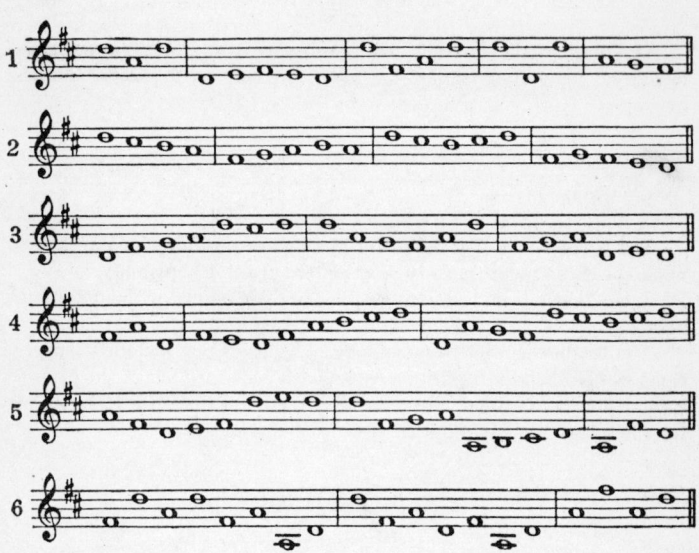

Harmonic:—

```
D  I³  I⁵  IV  I    V    V⁵  I
G  I³  IV  V   I    I³   IV  IV³  I
G  I³  V   I   IV   IV³  V   V⁵   I
A  I⁵  IV  IV⁵ V    V⁵   I   IV   I
E  I⁸  IV  V   I    I³   IV  V    I
E  I⁸  V   I   I³   IV   IV³ V    V³  I
```

LESSON 5

The Five Rules Let us now harmonize the melody, Ex. 8, at the keyboard in close position. As before, our vocabulary is I, IV, and V. We shall begin with I and choose the others by comparing the sound of the various possible solutions. Below the exercise the dash is used to indicate repetition of a chord. The last way is the best and from it we derive a few very important principles. These are best expressed in the form of five rules:—

Poorest	I	–	–	V	IV	I	V
Poor	I	–	–	–	IV	I	–
Good	I	IV	I	–	IV	V	I

Rule 1, the Common Tone A tone common to two successive chords is best kept in the same voice. The other voices move to the nearest chord tones.

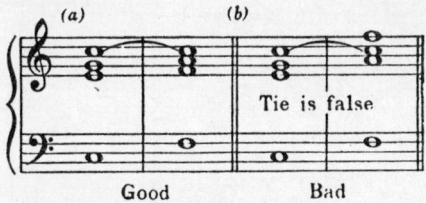

Rule 2, no Common Tone When there is no common tone, lead the upper three voices in contrary motion to the bass, to the nearest chord tones (*a*), to avoid parallel fifths and octaves which are forbidden (*b*). These occur when any two voices go

16   HARMONY FOR EAR, EYE, AND KEYBOARD

in the same direction a fifth or an octave apart. Parallel fifths are usually unpleasant, and parallel octaves interfere with the independence of some voice. Do not let the bass leap a seventh, as at (c).

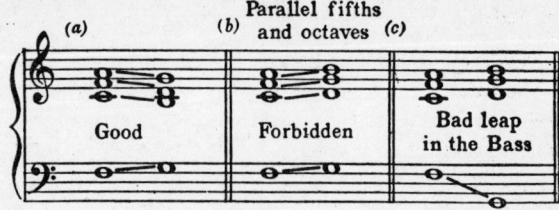

Rule 3, the Melody Repeats a Note   When the melody repeats a note, usually change the harmony (a). Exceptions to this are frequent in folk tunes, etc. (b):—

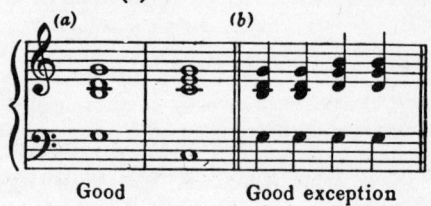

Rule 4, the Melody Leaps   When the melody leaps from one note to another of the same chord, do not change the harmony (a):—

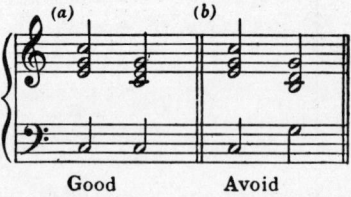

Rule 5, entering a New Measure   Change the harmony on entering a new measure (a). An exception to this is frequent where the melody begins on the last part of a measure (b):—

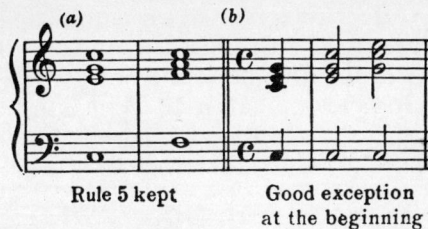

Rule 5 kept   Good exception at the beginning

After we have found the best solution of Ex. 8, have played it, and listened to it till we know it well, each one in the class may play two chords that illustrate, in turn, each of the five rules. Then these illustrations may be put on the board, the pupils working in groups of two or three if desired.

SIGHT-SINGING AND EAR-TRAINING

Spend half of the allotted time for this kind of work on singing melodies with the syllables. To lend interest and variety have one melody, or a set of melodies in the same key, sung by several people, each singing in turn but two measures, and losing no time between measures. The teacher will give the keynote only. Use no accompaniment. The student should learn to find any difficult interval by singing the scale-tones in between the two tones of the interval.

The following vocalises will be found just as helpful for the voice as five-finger exercises are for the piano student. Sing these, with the syllables, in all keys which lie within the range of the voices:—

HARMONY FOR EAR, EYE, AND KEYBOARD

Spend the remainder of the time on ear-training drill like that given in the last two lessons.

ASSIGNMENT

Keyboard Work: Illustrate at the piano and then at the board the common tone and also contrary motion where there is no common tone.
Harmonize Ex. 8 in the best way and transpose it to G, F#, and A. Harmonize the following: —

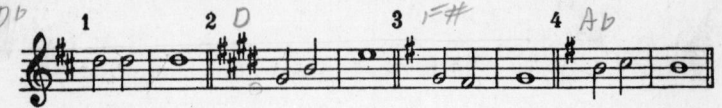

Written Work: Bring a solution of Ex. 8 in C and in two other keys (your choice). Use a tie to show where you keep the common tone; and, for a few lessons at least, the little lines to show the contrary motion where there is no common tone. Use close position this time in each exercise.

ADDITIONAL EXERCISES
(WRITTEN WORK)

LESSON 6

Interchange of Close and Open Position

Instead of writing all close position, or all open, it is better to follow the general principle that a high soprano invites open position and a low soprano close position. With a little soprano, like Ex. 8, the first three chords might well be open and the others close. Try it this way at the piano [Ex. 9 (*a*)]. Such interchange of position is frequent in music. Whenever you change from close position to open, or vice versa, do it while the harmony remains the same, if you can. Use care to retain all three tones of the triad in the upper three parts:—

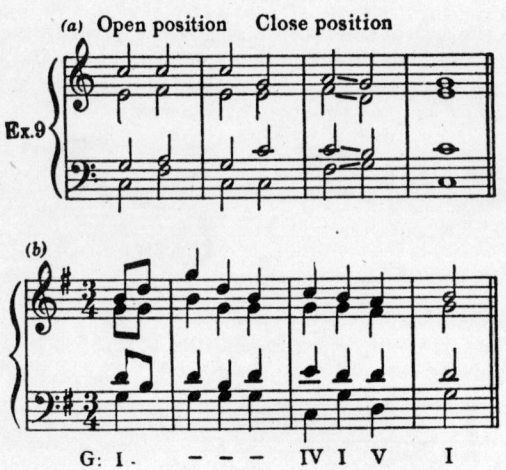

When a melody begins on an unaccented beat, it is usually best to keep the same harmony across the bar, as in Ex. 9 (*b*). (Cf. also Lesson 5, rule 5).

NOTATION

An examination of well edited music will prove that there are certain established customs in music notation. A knowledge of these is valuable. The more important points will be presented in this text as needed

Stems   When writing one part only on a staff follow these rules:—

1. If the note-head is below the third line, turn the stem up.
2. If the note-head is above the third line, turn the stem down.
3. If the note-head is on the third line, the stem may be turned in either direction, the choice depending on the symmetry of the melodic outline (1-4). In 3-4 note that when a melody begins with a note on the third line, as the last beat of a measure, its stem would better be turned in the same direction as that of the first note after the bar:—

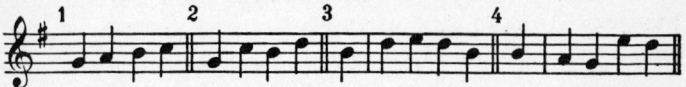

4. In the case of several stems stroked together, all may turn in one direction, the direction being determined by the majority of the note-heads (5-8):—

Notice in No. 8, the indication for a triplet is made next to the heads of the notes, and not against the stems.

The *dot* beside a note is always placed in a space, never on a line. In case the note is on a line, the position of the dot is determined by the following note (9-12):—

The teacher will dictate several melodies for practice in writing correctly. We shall speak of this kind of drill as "**Verbal Dictation.**" Use some of the material from the sight-singing book or any other similar material. An example follows:—

Teacher, "Key of D major. Four-quarter measure. Begin on low *do*. *Do, re, mi, fa,* quarters; *so* a half, *mi* a quarter, high *do, ti,* eighths stroked; *la* a dotted half, *ti* a quarter; *do* a whole note."

Solution:—

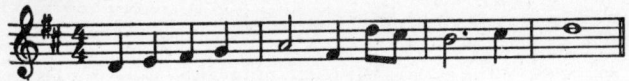

ASSIGNMENT

Keyboard Work: Invent four-measure exercises within your vocabulary.

Written Work: Transpose the soprano of Ex. 9 (*b*) to F♯, and harmonize it without the book. Harmonize the following melodies. Give the parts separate stems. Sing each melody over and plan the work, sketching in lightly the chord numbers you think will be best, and deciding where to carry the same harmony across the bar, the place for contrary motion, etc. As you put down the parts, think each one, as far as you have carried it, as though it were a singing voice:—

ADDITIONAL EXERCISES
(WRITTEN WORK)

LESSON 7

NOTATION (Con.)

Rests   The double-whole-rest, or breve, occasionally used, is a vertical whole-rest, filling the third space.

The whole-rest and the half-rest are each placed in the third space, the whole-rest being placed below the fourth line, the half-rest above the third line.

The rests of smaller denomination all occupy the middle two spaces of the staff. The quarter-rest is *not* a letter z. The eighth-rest suggests the figure 7 in appearance:—

Double-whole   Whole   Half   Quarter   Eighth   Sixteenth
or
Breve

It should be noted that the whole-rest may be used as a measure-rest, regardless of the measure sign (1). The whole-note may not be used in a similar way.

In case two or more parts are written on a staff, the position of the rests may vary:—

The *flags*, or hooks, of eighth and sixteenth notes are always placed on the right hand side of the stems, unless the stems are stroked together:—

The *tie* usually connects the heads of two notes. (Observe the notation of a first and second ending. The use of such endings often saves time in writing.):—

The teacher should now give some verbal dictation, in half-note and eighth-note notation, which will afford opportunity for practice on the preceding points.

Do not neglect the bass staff. For variety, dictate a few two-part exercises, similar to the following example, and have the class sing them. These will give excellent practice in sight-reading:—

From *Melodia, Bk I*, Cole and Lewis

SIGHT-SINGING

Spend any remaining time on sight-singing.

ASSIGNMENT

Keyboard Work: Harmonize the following:—

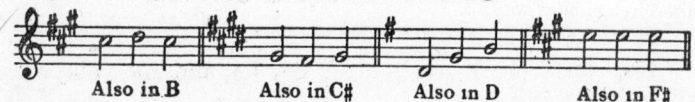

Written Work: **Review exercises.**
Using the primary triads and the suggestions in the preceding lessons, harmonize the following:—

LESSON 8

To Find the Keys in Flats — Apply the scale pattern as before, beginning on F, B♭, E♭, and A♭. Observe that the new flat is each time on four of the scale, and since these are a fourth apart we derive the following rule: **The fourth degree of any diatonic scale is the keynote of the following scale in flats (i. e., with one more flat).**

The flats are written in the signature in the order of their entry. The signatures of the first four flat keys are as follows:—

Ex 10 — F, B♭, E♭, A♭

Play the scale of triads in F, B♭, E♭, and A♭. Play in all positions as before.

Play the primary triads of each of these keys. Think and spell as accurately and quickly as you can. Be sure that you do not say *e–g–b* when you should say *e♭–g–b♭*. This is a matter in which you can not be too careful, for loose habits in spelling lead to inaccurate playing and writing.

Chord Repetition — In a simple study of chord connection it is usual to change the harmony (change to another chord) when a melody repeats a tone (Lesson 5). But in folk-songs, and music of a similar type, we find chord repetition under repeated melody notes wherever the composer chooses to use it for simple rhythmic interest. Compare the following (*a*) with its simple harmonic equivalent (*b*):—

Ex 11 *(a)* Chd. repetition *(b)* Har equivalent

While it may be interesting to harmonize a few melodies which lend themselves readily to chord repetition, you will see at once that, in point of time required, merely copying repeated chords is not the most direct way to study the connection of one chord with another. A good general principle to follow in this matter is to repeat the chord when the repeated melody notes are short and the change of harmony would make the passage heavy (look for repeated chords in any book of part songs). For instance, in the following examples the first is far the better: —

Ex 12 *(a)* Allegro *(b)*
Good Poor

SIGHT-READING AND EAR-TRAINING

A good collection of folk-songs, arranged for part-singing, should be in every school library.

Select two songs, perhaps "Battle Hymn of the Republic" and "Juanita." Have the class sing with the syllables the bass part, then the alto, of the first. Of the second, sing the bass, tenor, and alto in turn; and then all four parts unaccompanied. Whenever the student has an opportunity to hear part-singing, he should listen to the lower parts, learn to follow them, and not always confine his attention to the soprano.

Spend about two minutes analyzing chord position by ear.

26 HARMONY FOR EAR, EYE, AND KEYBOARD

ASSIGNMENT

Keyboard Work: Play the major scales of F, B♭, E♭ and A♭.
  Play the scale of triads in each of these keys, and in the usual three positions.
  Play the primary triads of these keys.

Written Work: Write the scales of F, B♭, E♭ and A♭ major.
  Harmonize the following melodies: —

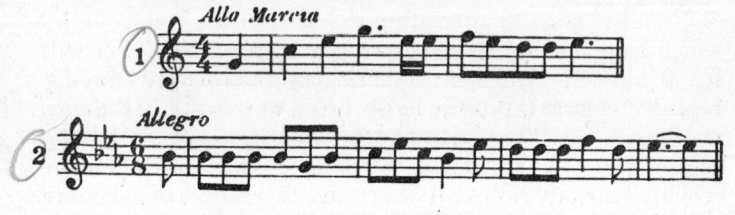

ADDITIONAL EXERCISES
(NOTATION)

Verbal Dictation:—

LESSON 9

The remaining scales in flats, D♭, G♭, and C♭, should now be learned. Play the scale, the scale of chords, and the primary triads in each of these keys. Here follow their signatures:—

Ex 13

Harmonizing 1-2 of the Scale   Thus far we have obeyed the rule for keeping a common tone in the same voice, but in the progression of the soprano from *one to two* of the scale, and also from *two to one*, the rule is freely broken provided the upper three voices are led in contrary motion to the bass. This enables us to harmonize easily in the scale 1–2–3–4–3–2–1, keeping everywhere the common tone except between 1–2 or 2–1.

Try this on the piano. Play the progression in several keys; listen to it; commit it to memory, for you will find many passages of melody where you can use the chords in this way. See Ex. 14 (*a*), (*b*):—

Ex.14

EAR-TRAINING

Melodic: The class will first sing each of the following melodies with the book open; then without the book, to see whether it is correctly memorized. Next, write it on the music tablet, and finally compare it with the book:—

The following melodies will be played by the teacher and sung from memory by the pupils. They will then write as before and compare with the book. When mistakes are made, the pupil may sing his incorrect solution and compare the sound with the original melody:—

Harmonic: Spend perhaps two minutes on the primary triads, analyzing them by ear. Always analyze the position of the first triad in an exercise. This can be indicated by 1^3, 1^5, or 1^8, the small number indicating 3rd, 5th, or 8ve in the soprano.

ASSIGNMENT

Keyboard Work: Play the scales of D♭, G♭, and C♭ major.
Play the scale of chords and the primary triads in each of these keys as before.
Harmonize *do—re—do* in every key in flats.

Written Work: Write the scales of D♭, G♭ and C♭ major.
Harmonize the following:—

LESSON 10

Intervals An *Interval* is the relation which one tone sustains to another with regard to pitch.

Intervals are always reckoned upward unless otherwise stated. The number name is determined by the number of staff degrees, inclusive, embraced by the notes of the interval. We say *Prime* instead of *First*. Intervals larger than an octave are the Ninth, Tenth, Eleventh, and so on; but a Ninth is usually treated as a Second, a Tenth as a Third, etc.

In the major scale, reckoning from the keynote, the intervals are as follows: —

Ex. 15

Perfect prime	Major second	Major third	Perfect fourth	Perfect fifth	Major sixth	Major seventh	Perfect octave
P.P.	Ma.2	Ma.3	P.4	P.5	Ma.6	Ma.7	P.8

Abbreviation:

To Read Intervals This model forms the measurement basis for reading intervals easily and rapidly. If the upper note is 1, 4, 5, or 8 in the scale of the lower the interval is perfect; and if 2, 3, 6, or 7, it is major. For example, a perfect fourth from G is C because C is 4 in the scale of G; a major third from D is F♯ because F♯ is 3 in the scale of D, etc. To read intervals, therefore, you should consider the lower note the keynote of the major scale. By the same process, play major and perfect intervals from any letter. Also, name them when played, thus keeping the ear in active co-operation.

Minor Intervals A *Minor Interval* is the interval next smaller than major, the letter names remaining the same; e. g., C–E is a major third; C–E♭ or C♯–E, a minor third. Perfect intervals have no minor form.

Inversion of Intervals
An interval is *inverted* when the relative position of the two notes is changed by placing one of them an octave higher or lower than before.

Perfect intervals when inverted remain perfect, *either tone is in the major scale of the other*; but: major intervals when inverted become minor and minor intervals become major. For example, invert all the intervals in Ex. 15 by placing the C up an octave, and we have a perfect octave in place of the perfect prime, a minor seventh in place of the major second, etc. Name the other inversions in this way.

Major and Minor Triads
Major and *minor thirds* are very important intervals, for they are used in building chords.

A *Major Triad* has a *major third* and a perfect fifth (reckoned from its root).

A *Minor Triad* has a *minor third* and a perfect fifth.

The fifth is the same in either case. It is the *third* which makes the triad major or minor.

Now you may play major thirds from dictation, changing each to minor. Spell. Play major triads and change them to minor in the same way.

SIGHT-SINGING AND EAR-TRAINING

Vocalize in thirds.

Tonal Ear-Training: The teacher will play, *once only*, groups of tones which include the leap of a third. Class write.

Intervals: Play major and minor thirds, seconds, and sevenths for the class to compare and analyze by ear. (Sixths are purposely omitted until later. Thirds should receive the greatest emphasis.)

Triads: Use the neutral syllable *la*, not the syllable names.

Sing a major triad above a given tone and then make it minor. Reverse this order.

Analyze triads as the teacher plays them, testing the third with the voice whenever in doubt as to the "color" of the triad.

ASSIGNMENT

Keyboard Work: Play major triads anywhere on the keyboard and change each to minor. Play minor triads and change them to major. Play major and minor thirds and triads, spelling each.

Written Work: Write and name all the perfect and major intervals from E♭ and B, using Ex. 15 as a model. Write the following triads by adding the proper third and fifth to the given root: —

ADDITIONAL EXERCISES
(ORAL WORK)

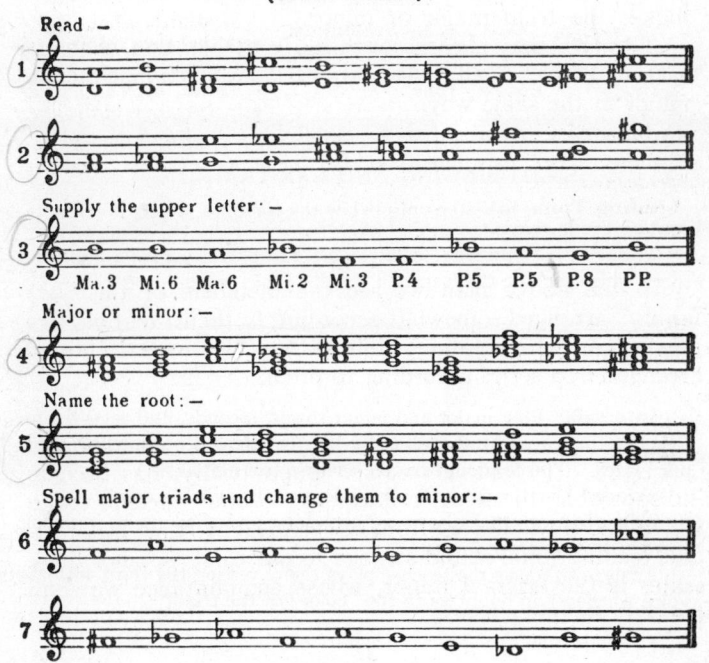

LESSON 11

Special Names of Members of Key
Each tone of a key has a special name as follows: I, *Tonic*; II, *Supertonic*; III, *Mediant*; IV, *Subdominant*; V, *Dominant*; VI, *Submediant*; VII, *Leading Tone*.
Chords formed on these degrees take the same names. We therefore say "tonic chord" "dominant chord," etc. These names should be memorized by noting their relation to the tonic, as follows: —

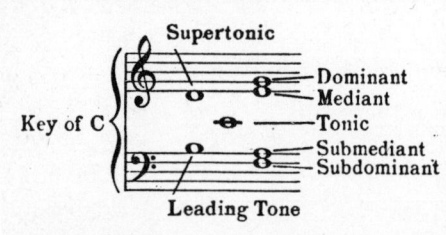

Key of C — Supertonic, Dominant, Mediant, Tonic, Submediant, Subdominant, Leading Tone.

Supertonic, from its position next above the tonic.
Dominant, most important after the tonic.
Mediant, about halfway between tonic and dominant.
Tonic, or keynote, principal tone of the key.
Submediant, about halfway between tonic and underdominant.
Subdominant, most important after the dominant, also called the *underdominant*.
Leading Tone, half-step only below the tonic, to which it strongly *leads*.

In the above plan we see the members of the "key family" arranged somewhat according to their function, like players ready for a game; while in the scale we see the family arranged in a series according to pitch.

Leading Tone The *Leading Tone*, so near to the tonic and leading to it so emphatically, has become indispensable to modern harmony. Some ancient scales which had a whole step from seven to eight (thus lacking a true leading tone) sound strange to our ears. One of these scales is the original minor, whose acquaintance we shall make in the next lesson.

Minor Triads on I and IV in Minor Keys

Thus far you have used only major triads, the tonic, the dominant, and the subdominant, in harmonizing the little melodies in previous lessons. Let us turn back to Ex. 5 (*a*) and play it in minor; that is, make each triad minor. Play it again, allowing V to remain major. Note how much more satisfactory this last is to our ears. The ear demands a *leading tone*, a half-step below the tonic. In minor then, we shall use a minor triad on I and IV, and a major triad on V. (Notice the small numerals for minor triads.) It is very important to remember that this triad on V (the dominant), whether in a major key or a minor key, is *always major*.

SIGHT-SINGING AND EAR-TRAINING

The teacher will play exercises, similar to the above, in several keys and the class will analyze by answering, "mediant, dominant, supertonic, etc." Also sing these with the syllable names. Give further drill of this sort after the following discussion of the scale tones.

Now listen to the character of each of these scale tones:

Do, mi, so. Each of these may be used as a tone of repose at the close of a melody; *do*, the keynote, being most conclusive. All are members of the tonic chord.

Ti, fa, re, la. Sing *ti*, the leading tone, and feel its strong tendency to do. *Fa* has nearly as pronounced a tendency downward to *mi*. *Re* and *la* are not tones of repose but their tendency depends much on their place in the melodic phrase, or in the chord.

La, in the minor key, is *tonic* and therefore has all the qualities of repose possessed by any tonic.

While any tendency tone may be passed through degreewise in either direction, it is very desirable that a constantly increasing sense of tendency and repose values in the tones of the scale should be thoughtfully cultivated.

The following vocal exercise is to be practised daily outside of class. The pupil will test at the piano occasionally to see whether he is singing in tune:—

34 HARMONY FOR EAR, EYE, AND KEYBOARD

Sight-Singing: A few minutes devoted to something in which *thirds* are plentiful.

ASSIGNMENT

Keyboard Work: Play the first few exercises in your blank book in minor instead of in major.
  Play major and minor thirds and triads, spelling each.

Written Work: Harmonize the following:—

ADDITIONAL EXERCISES
(WRITTEN WORK)

LESSON 12

Minor Scale Original Form

The white keys on the piano from A to A represent a typical *Minor Scale* in its *Original Form*. Listen to it and observe its pattern. The half-steps occur between 2⌣3 and 5⌣6: 1—2⌣3—4—5⌣6—7—8.

The chief characteristic of a minor scale is the *Minor Third* from 1 to 3.

Relative Keys

Relative Keys are those which have the same signature. C major and *a* minor are therefore relative keys. In other words, *a* minor is the relative minor of C major. Their relation to each other is shown in the following example: —

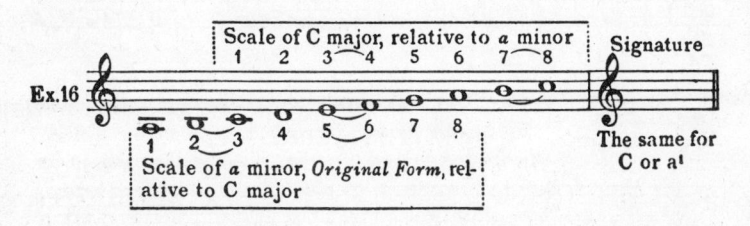

Ex. 16 [musical staff: Scale of C major, relative to *a* minor, 1 2 3⌣4 5 6 7⌣8; Scale of *a* minor, *Original Form*, relative to C major, 1 2⌣3 4 5⌣6 7 8; Signature: The same for C or a[1]]

Play (and spell) the relative minor scale, original form, of any major scale. Observe that you simply play each major scale from its sixth degree, but that this degree is now a *tonic* (first degree) in the minor scale. The keynote of the relative minor is a *minor third below* the keynote of its relative major, and the keynote of the relative major, a *minor third above* the keynote of its relative minor.

Primary Triads in Minor

We have already played major exercises in minor by using minor chords. Now let us form the three primary triads (tonic, dominant, and subdominant) in the key of *a* minor. Derived

[1] A small letter indicates minor.

from the original form of the minor scale, each has a minor third and a perfect fifth, so they are minor chords. Used in a short phrase they appear as in Ex. 17 (a):—

Primary triads formed from the original form of minor scale.   Primary triads formed from the harmonic form of minor scale.

Ex 17

Because our ears crave a Leading Tone (the g♯)

a: i iv i V i   i iv i V i

Small numerals because the triads are minor.   A large numeral for the dominant triad because it is now a major triad.

Origin of the Harmonic Form The original form of the minor scale was adequate to the needs of very early music, in fact it is one of several ancient scales used in the church before harmony, as we know it, was developed. But with the introduction of part-singing, the need of a leading tone, as in the major scale, became so evident to both singers and composers, that it was introduced to make a good close. Later, instead of using the "raised seven" at the close only, it was added throughout the piece in whatever chord *seven of the scale* appeared. Thus the pattern of our present *Harmonic Minor Scale* was determined. No change in the signature is involved, but seven of the scale is chromatically raised.

Compare Ex. 17 (a) and (b) at the piano and you will see that, whereas in the last lesson you changed major exercises to minor by using minor chords on I and IV, you now derive your minor tonality from chords built *in the minor key*. Reversing the process of last lesson, you can play Ex. 17 in major by simply changing every chord to major, but do not confuse this with the *relative major key*. The keys of *a minor* and *A major* are not relatives but two different modes whose keynotes are identical (homonymic keys).

Augmented Second from 6 to 7

The *harmonic form* of the *minor scale* should be learned as thoroughly as the major scale. The step-and-a-half (called an augmented second) between 6-7 is unvocal and a source of some trouble to the beginner, but the gain in having a leading tone, and thereby obtaining a major triad on V, is so great that we keep this form and find ways to disguise its defects. In writing this scale use (+) to indicate the position of the step-and-a-half. Alphabetical order is necessary, hence *g* should not be written for *f*×.

EAR-TRAINING

Triads: Spend two minutes analyzing major and minor triads by ear.
Intervals: The class will differentiate between major and minor sixths as they are played. The major sixth sounds like low *so* up to *mi*, in the major scale — or, possibly, *do* up to *la*; the minor sixth sounds like *mi* up to high *do*.
Verbal Dictation: The teacher will dictate syllable names rather rapidly (15 to 20 in each exercise) and the class will write whole-notes on the staff as fast as dictated. Use the bass staff a part of the time.

ASSIGNMENT

Keyboard Work: Play and spell the original form of each minor scale in sharps, then change each to harmonic form.
Play the primary triads in e, b, and f♯, using the harmonic form only.
Written Work: Write the minor scales, harmonic form, in sharps, according to the following model: —

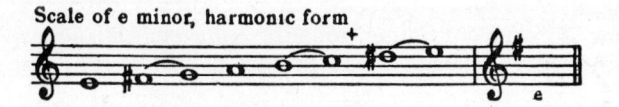

38　　HARMONY FOR EAR, EYE, AND KEYBOARD

Harmonize. Mark V large, the other chords small:—

Key of *a* minor

ADDITIONAL EXERCISES
(WRITTEN WORK)

(EAR-TRAINING)

Intervals:— Name as played

Triads:— Major or minor; 8, 5, or 3 in the soprano?

Tonal:—

LESSON 13

SIGHT-READING AND EAR-TRAINING

Melodic: The class will sing and write from memory after hearing each melody played twice.

The teacher will encourage memorizing groups of tones rather than individual tones. Notice that the first melody divides naturally by measures. The second, though longer, is easily memorized if correctly grouped because of its repetition. The first two measures are repeated; the sixth measure is the fifth a step higher, and the seventh consists of thirds. The attention should center on the first tone in measures five, six, and seven: —

Folk-Songs: Have the class sing the lower parts of several folk-songs, as in Lesson 8. Suggestions:

"Old Folks at Home"   "Old Black Joe"
"Come, Thou Almighty King"   "Silent Night"

Intervals:

The teacher will first play the two tones of the interval consecutively, the lower tone first; then play simultaneously. It is understood that no interval except those presented in Lesson 10 will be played. Pupils will analyze as fast as played, saying, "major third, minor second, major sixth, etc."

Now play the first interval (major third) and have the class sing the minor third; play the second interval (minor second) and have the class sing the major second, etc., of course omitting the perfect intervals. Do not name the interval played.

ASSIGNMENT

Keyboard Work: Play and spell the original form of each minor scale in flats, then change each to harmonic form.
Play the primary triads in d, g, c, and f, using the harmonic form only.

Written Work: Write the minor scales, harmonic form, in flats. Harmonize:—

ADDITIONAL EXERCISES
(WRITTEN WORK)

(EAR-TRAINING)

Melodic:—

LESSON 14

Cadences A *Cadence* is the close of a musical phrase, and is formed by the last two (or more) chords.

An *Authentic Cadence* is formed by the progression V–I.
A *Plagal Cadence* is formed by the progression IV–I.

These cadences are *perfect* when the soprano ends on the root of the last chord, and *imperfect* when it does not. Play the following models and transpose them to other keys:—

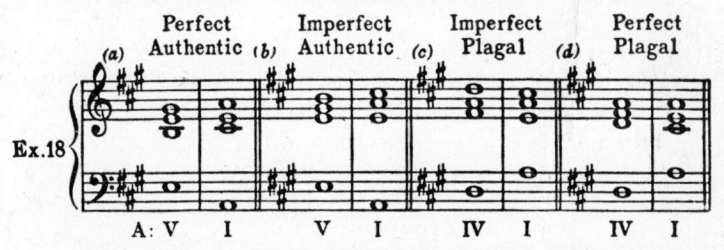

Ex.18

(a) Perfect Authentic (b) Imperfect Authentic (c) Imperfect Plagal (d) Perfect Plagal

A: V I   V I   IV I   IV I

A *Half Cadence* is formed by ending a phrase on V. This is equivalent to the rising inflection in speech and occurs where a partial close is appropriate.

The Period In the following model, Ex. 19, the first four measures (called the *Thesis*) close with a *half cadence* that, like a question, causes us to expect an answering phrase (*Antithesis*) which closes with a perfect cadence. Such a musical sentence is called a *Period*:—

Ex.19

Thesis _____   Half Cadence

I   V

Change all the cadences in Ex. 18 to minor. Play Ex.19 in minor.

SIGHT-SINGING AND EAR-TRAINING

Sight-Singing: About half of the allotted time. Use a few melodies for practice in memorizing.

Triads: Analyze both color and position. (About two minutes.)

Intervals: See Lesson 13. (About two minutes.)

Harmonic: Play cadences, as illustrated in this lesson, and have the class name them. Play one or two in minor.

ASSIGNMENT

Keyboard Work: Play authentic and plagal cadences, both perfect and imperfect, in G, D♭, A, and F, and in c, f♯, and e. Bring to class an illustration of each cadence from your practical music or from a book of hymn tunes.

Written Work: Harmonize the following, and name each cadence. Add an *Antithesis* (four measures) to No. 3 and close it with a plagal cadence: —

LESSON 15[1]

Ear-Training Review Give a test representative of the various kinds of work touched upon thus far. The difficulty will depend upon the ability of the particular group of students. The following points might well be included: —

   Verbal Dictation: Testing knowledge of notation.
   Melodic: Tonal groups, melodies.
   Harmonic: Primary triads, cadences, intervals, triad position, and color.

Keyboard Work Review Give a test on the various forms of keyboard work, three or four minutes being allowed for each pupil.. The teacher should keep the difficulty of this work well within the ability of the student, make no comment on his recitation while he is playing, and then pass quickly to the next pupil. The following is suggestive merely: —

[2]First pupil: Major scale of E; G I[a]–V–I; D perfect plagal cadence;

Second pupil: Major scale of B; transpose Ex. 7 in text to D; play the primary triads in e minor.

Third pupil: Play B♭ I[a]–IV–I; invent four measures closing with V–I.

Fourth pupil: Harmonize ; transpose it to three other keys. Play and spell the scale of d minor, harmonic form.

Fifth pupil: Invent four measures closing with IV–I; scale of A♭; play major triads on E, D, F♯, and change to minor.

Sixth pupil; Harmonize E♭; scale of triads in G at the top. ; transpose it to with the thirds

---
[1]If desired, two or three sessions might be devoted to this review lesson.
[2] The figure 3, 5, or 8 used with the first chord-numeral will indicate that the soprano should begin on the 3rd, 5th, or 8ve respectively.

44 HARMONY FOR EAR, EYE, AND KEYBOARD

Seventh pupil: Scale of triads in D with roots at the top; major thirds on E, B♭, A, and change to minor; original form of e minor scale, spell and change to harmonic form.

Eighth pupil: Harmonize *do-re-do* in F; change Ex. 7 to minor; play the primary triads in b minor.

Ninth pupil: Play three minor triads anywhere and change them to major; perfect authentic cadence in A; play the same in a.

Tenth pupil: Scale of triads in G♭ with the fifths at the top; harmonize (selected exercise   ); change a major exercise to minor by the teacher from the pupil's book).

Written Work Review The following exercises are selected with especial reference to the vocabulary, I–IV–V, root position, and the requirements of the preceding lessons. To select an average lesson of three exercises choose one from the first five, one from the second, and one from the third: —

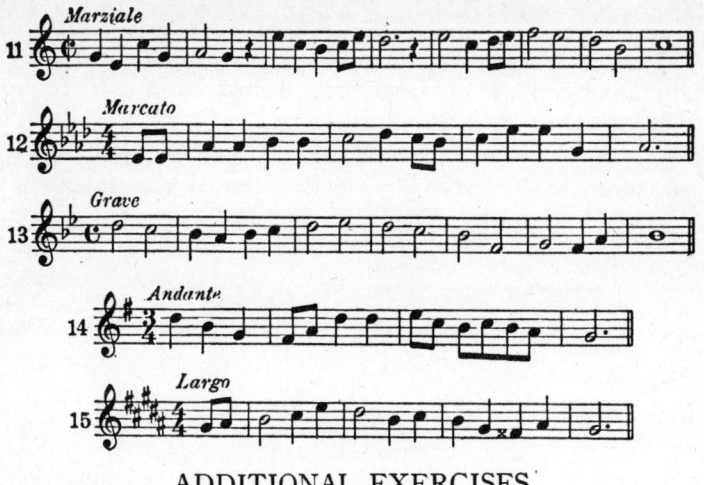

ADDITIONAL EXERCISES
(EAR-TRAINING)

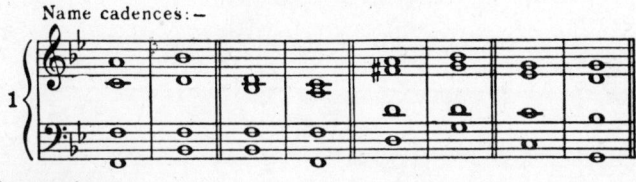

Name cadences:—

Harmonic:—

Tonal:—

LESSON 16

Figured Bass
Its Origin
About 1600 A. D., when opera was first written and the composer needed a sort of musical shorthand by which to indicate his score, without writing out all the parts, *Figured Bass* (or *Thorough Bass*) was invented and came rapidly into general use. By this system, only the bass notes were written, with figures to indicate the other tones. From such a figured bass alone, an organist could reproduce the composer's idea and could accompany recitative, songs, and choruses, or even play an elaborate organ part along with the orchestra, thus saving an enormous amount of copying. For more than a century this system served the composer well; but the increasing complexity of his scores forced him to an exact reproduction of his music, with the result that he was eventually compelled to write out in full every part. Finally, accompanying from figured bass fell into disuse.

Present Value
For those who study harmony, figured (and unfigured) bass still renders a valuable service and forms a part of the student's training in practically every great conservatory of music in the world. Its brevity and definiteness, its friendly challenge to the student to realize musically the composer's idea, in fact, its many sided musical problem in fashioning the progress of the upper voices and crowning the whole with the most melodious soprano possible — all these combine to make it highly valuable. It provides, moreover, a means of increasing the student's vocabulary. It suggests successions and arrangements of chords which would scarcely occur to the unaided beginner, and his solutions must be determined by a process of interval analysis of value throughout his course.

Sources
A wealth of figured bass exists, prepared by great musicians from Bach down to the present day. As soon as the student is ready for moderately

advanced work, he will find the great collections used in such conservatories as those in Paris, Moscow, London, and Berlin a spur to still further study (See Appendix A, div. VI).

The Meaning of the Figures The figures always indicate what intervals are to be reckoned *from the bass note* over (or under) which they appear. For example, in the root position of a triad, no matter how the upper voices are arranged, the only possible intervals *from the bass* are the 8ve, 5th, and 3rd. Hence used singly, or in combination with each other, 8, 5, and 3 always indicate that the bass is the root of a triad. The figure 3, or no figure, is most usual:—

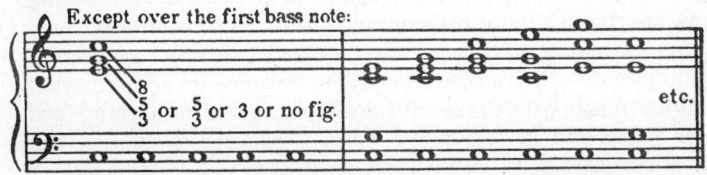

Except over the first bass note:

$\frac{8}{5}$ or $\frac{5}{3}$ or 3 or no fig.

The root position of a triad is indicated in any of these ways.   And may be arranged in any of these ways.

Over the first bass note of an exercise, 8, 5, or 3, while retaining its original function, indicates that the soprano is to begin on the 8ve, 5th, or 3rd, respectively. If there is no figure over this first note, an 8 is usually understood. After this first note these figures do not apply to the soprano:—

Over the first bass note

No figure or 8 means this or this | 5 this or this | 3 this or this

A (♯), (♭), or (♮), standing alone over a bass note, refers to the third above that note (an abbreviation of 3♯, 3♭, 3♮). If any other interval is to be altered the proper figure is used with the sign; e. g., 8♭, 5♭, 6♯, etc.

Inversion of Triads A triad is *inverted* when, in place of the root, the bass is the third or the fifth.

The *Chord of the Sixth* is a triad with its third in the bass (the first inversion). In a figured bass this is indicated by a figure 6 because the root is then a sixth above the bass.

In a chord of the sixth double the root or fifth; *not the bass*, for it is the third and will be unpleasantly prominent if doubled. (The third of a chord is doubled under certain circumstances to be considered later.)

The *Six-four Chord* is a triad with its fifth in the bass (the second inversion). In a figured bass this is indicated by the figures $^6_4$ because the other tones are a sixth and a fourth above the bass. In a six-four chord always double the bass note, the fifth.

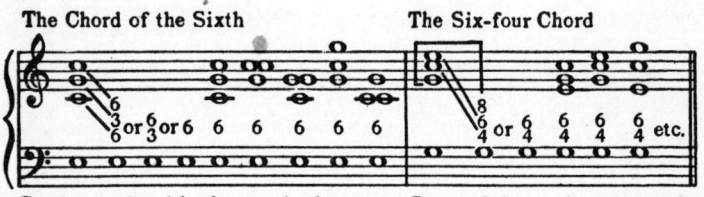

Can be arranged in these and other ways. Some of the good arrangements.

EAR-TRAINING

Key and Interval Drill: Dictation similar to the following: Give the tone D. Ask the class to sing *do, re, mi*; call the last tone *la* and sing *la, ti, do*; call that tone *fa* and sing *fa, mi, re, do*. What key? (Answer E). Test at the piano to see whether the class is in tune.

Note—A stroke through a figure is sometimes used to indicate elevation a chromatic half-step; e. g., 6̶ = 6♯; but this is not recommended.

Tonal Drill: The teacher will play groups of five to seven tones, including leaps to tendency tones. Class write after one hearing: —

Harmonic: The teacher will play a single chord. One pupil will analyze the chord and another write it out in full at the board with the correct figuring. Each chord is a separate problem:—

ASSIGNMENT

Keyboard Work: Play the tonic triad of C major (four part) in root position, then as a chord of the sixth, last as a six-four chord. Do the same with D I, E♭ I, etc. Treat minor triads in the same way. Bring in examples of 6 and $\frac{6}{4}$ from practical music.

Written Work: Supply the upper three parts to the following figured bass notes. Give four different arrangements of each chord over the last five notes. Be sure to double the proper chord tone: —

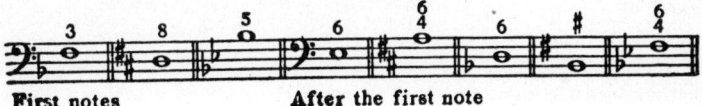

First notes   **After the first note**

LESSON 17

The Six-Four Chord

To alter slightly a familiar jingle, we may say of the six-four chord, that "Where it is good, it is very, very good; and where it is bad, it is horrid." Its use is very restricted. It is pre-eminently a cadencing chord and, as such, will be limited at present to the following conditions: —

Position in the Cadence

1. It must be a *tonic six-four, on an accent, in the cadence.*
2. The root and third descend stepwise into the next chord which should be V.

Ex 20

EAR-TRAINING

Harmonic: The teacher will play Ex. 20 and have the class analyze each chord and name the cadences.

Also play exercises similar to the following (no inversions) and have the class write out on staff paper the soprano, bass, and the chord numerals. The first time emphasize the soprano, the second time emphasize the bass, then play once or twice with no particular emphasis, giving the class an opportunity to hear the chord color and the chord successions as a whole:—

ASSIGNMENT

Keyboard Work: Play Ex. 20; note the balance between the two halves of the period, and test by ear the cadencing force of each of the six-four chords. Play this in B♭, and D.

Written Work: Harmonize this soprano, using two tonic six-four chords:—

Also compose an original in G. Mark off the eight measures first, then sketch in the two cadences so as to make a period similar to Ex. 20. Select your material (aside from the cadences) from the primary triads and plan your melody as in previous lessons.

LESSON 18

The Chord of the Sixth

The primary triads may all be used in the form of Chords of the Sixth. We now have the first real opportunity to give the bass some melodic character. Thus far all the bass could do was to leap stiffly from one root to another every time the chord changed. No wonder if you began to feel sorry for it. Sing the following bass, note its increased flexibility, and let us work it out together:—

Fig. Bass

Solution

I I^6 I V^6 I IV^6 I I$^6_4$ V$^5_3$ I I$_6$ IV I$_6$ I IV I$^6_4$ V^3 I

At (*a*) the figure 3 makes the soprano begin on the third.

At (*b*) the soprano doubles the root in unison with the alto. It could be C instead, but at a loss to the melody if C is to be taken in the second measure.

At (*c*) the soprano doubles the root in the octave with the tenor. This C is in the next chord (common tone). When we can keep a common tone in either the soprano, or in a middle voice, we usually keep it in the latter and let the soprano move.

At (*d*) the soprano and tenor again double the root. From here to the next chord the soprano could have gone up to C, the tenor down to A, but as we have it the melody is better.

At (e) we conform to the conditions applying to the six-four chord. From here on the class may consider this an "injured manuscript." In groups of two or three take it to the blackboard and "restore it."

SIGHT-SINGING AND EAR-TRAINING

Sight-Singing: If the pupil will notice how melodies are constructed he will later be able to invent some of his own. While singing, note any period forms, tonal or rhythmic repetition, sequence, etc.

Sequence — One or more repetitions of a short melodic figure at a higher or lower pitch forms a *Melodic Sequence:*—

Harmonic: The pupil will write the soprano, bass, and chord numerals, as in Lesson 17. Then analyze orally as it is played once again without reference to the paper:—

I^8 I^6 - V V^6 I I^6 IV I_4^6 V   I

I^8 I^6 IV IV^6 IV^8 I_4^6 V   I

ASSIGNMENT

Keyboard Work: Play the following in several major keys:—

Written Work: Supply the middle voices in No. 1, and harmonize No. 2, seeking the very best soprano possible. Figure the chords as usual, remembering that the *Roman numerals always refer to roots*:—

ADDITIONAL EXERCISES
(WRITTEN WORK)

LESSON 19

The Six-Four Chord and Chord of the Sixth (Con.)

Freedom in the choice and use of inversions comes only with practice and thoughtful analysis of good models. With nothing but the primary triads, in root position, we needed scarcely any help beyond the little rules in Lesson 5. Now we must consider the following:—

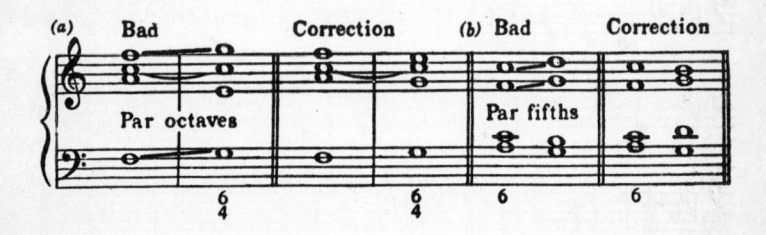

At (*a*) we have parallel octaves even though there be a common tone. The tenor makes an unnecessary leap down to E. In the correction the soprano takes E, tenor G, and the octaves disappear (Lesson 5, rule 1).

At (*b*) bad parallel fifths occur between the soprano and alto, a new problem, not covered by any rule so far. The fifths disappear if we lead the soprano to B, the tenor to D. This is sometimes called "mixed motion." No rule. It is sufficient to observe such cases.

EAR-TRAINING

Key and Interval Drill, as in Lesson 16.

Melodic: Insist upon accurate rests. Note the use of the sequence.

ASSIGNMENT

Keyboard Work: Play the following in several other minor keys. If it needs an answering phrase can you supply it?

Written Work: Harmonize the following, taking care to choose inversions in No. 2 that will enable you to write a good bass:—

ADDITIONAL EXERCISES

(WRITTEN WORK)

LESSON 20

Passing Tones We have now reached a good place to begin to use the passing tones. *Passing tones* are tones unessential to the harmony with which they appear, introduced stepwise between consecutive harmony notes. We are defining the simplest form and will confine their use to the soprano in this lesson. Furthermore, to keep the harmony clear the passing tones will appear on the unaccented beat (or portion of a beat) and be marked with (+). Example 21 should be played, analyzed by both ear and eye, and transposed to several other keys:—

Ex. 21

Oblique motion into a unison.

At (*a*) and (*b*) are passing tones which move away from the adjacent voice (alto). These are the easiest to manage.

At (*c*) is a passing tone that moves toward the adjacent voice. This is good if there is room to avoid such a progression as is shown at (*d*).

At (*d*) is a bad place for a passing tone. It must not move obliquely into a unison.

Kinds of Motion The kinds of motion between any two voices are usually classified as follows:

Parallel, same direction at the same interval distance.
Similar, same direction but not necessarily parallel.
Oblique, one voice moves, the other remains stationary.
Contrary, both parts move in opposite directions.

Third Doubled or Omitted A chord well defined and with the proper tone doubled on an accented beat (or part of a beat) may have its third doubled, or omitted, on the immediately following weak beat or part of a beat. This applies as well to its other tones. See Ex. 22 (*a*), (*b*). At (*c*) the triad is satisfactory with no fifth till the second beat. We could not omit the third on an accent like this. All these should be justified through some compensating gain in the melodic character of the flowing part, as in the following example where momentary doubling or omission is quite secondary to the importance of gaining a flexible soprano: —

Ex. 22

EAR-TRAINING

Tonal: —

Interval drill, as in Lesson 13.
Melodic: —

Assuming that the pupils were to harmonize the above melodies, let them sketch in the chord numerals and mark any passing tones.

ASSIGNMENT

Keyboard Work: Play Ex. 22 as it stands; then play it omitting each passing tone. Try it also in F in the two ways.

Written Work: Rewrite the following, introducing appropriate passing tones in the soprano:—

Supply the middle voices according to the figured bass, number the chords, and put a (+) over each passing tone:—

ADDITIONAL EXERCISES

(WRITTEN WORK)

LESSON 21

Accented Passing Tones

Accented Passing Tones connect chord tones in much the same way as do those we have just been using but they must be employed sparingly or the harmony will be blurred. Like a pungent flavor "just enough" is plenty. It is usual to distinguish these from the unaccented passing tones with (o). See Ex. 23.

Embellishment

An *Embellishment* is similar to a passing tone except that it returns to the tone whence it came. It can be accented or unaccented and, in either case, is marked with the letter E.

We must not attempt any extensive study of these ornaments now, but a "bowing acquaintance" with them will make some other things much easier to understand; as, for example, some other six-four chords in the next lesson. Notice the three kinds of ornaments in the following:—

EAR-TRAINING

Melodic:—

62 HARMONY FOR EAR, EYE, AND KEYBOARD

Harmonic: Note the passing tones and embellishments in the above melodies, considering but one chord to each measure.

The teacher will play any of the harmony exercises in Lessons 18-20 and have the class analyze them by ear.

ASSIGNMENT

Keyboard Work: Play the following as it stands, then play it omitting the passing tones. Play it in C, D, and A in the same way:—

Written Work: Harmonize the following, figure the chords, and indicate the passing tones and embellishments. As in Lesson 20 use the nonharmonic tones in the soprano only:—

LESSON 22

Some Other Six-Four Chords

The best six-four chord is unquestionably the accented I_4^6 in the authentic, and the half cadence (Lesson 17), but there are two other six-four chords whose names betray their derivation from the embellishment and the passing tone. These chords will be used as follows:

Embellishing Six-Four

Embellishing six-four (accented or unaccented) the bass remaining stationary on the tonic or the dominant. No voice leaps either to or from the six-four. The voices that move behave like embellishments which they really are (*a*), (*b*).

Passing Six-Four

Passing six-four (unaccented) connecting I with I^6, or IV with IV^6. No voice leaps. The fifths of the six-four are really passing tones, the third is an embellishment (*c*), (*d*).

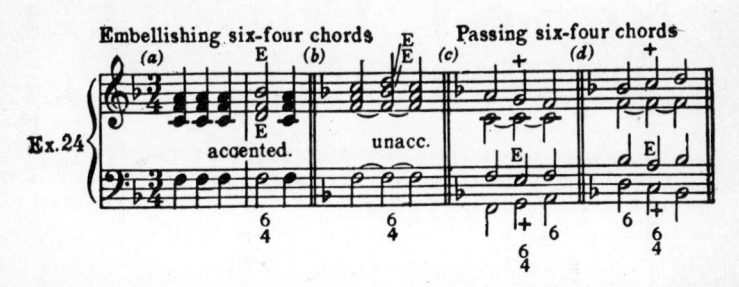

Ex. 24

Ornamenting the Plagal Cadence

Still another six-four (accented IV_4^6) ornaments the plagal cadence very much as the I_4^6 is used in the half cadence. This, like all other six-fours, results from the employment of some form of ornament, a full discussion of which does not belong in elementary work.

64   HARMONY FOR EAR, EYE, AND KEYBOARD

Ex. 25 — Ornamented Plagal Cadences

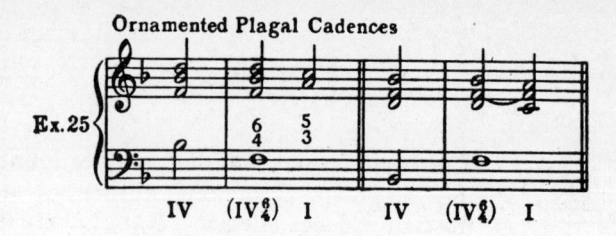

IV (IV$^6_4$) I   IV (IV$^6_4$) I

EAR-TRAINING

Melodic: Write the tune of "America" from memory (key G). Test any doubtful spot by singing the syllables. Sing each measure containing this rhythm ♩. ♪ and make the dot audible by a little emphasis or pulsation of the voice. Clap this rhythm while counting "one, two, three" and be sure that the hands do not make a sound as the "two" is voiced.

Clapping or tapping is extremely good rhythmic drill. Let the left hand keep a steady beat, like a metronome, and with the right hand tap rhythmic exercises such as the following. This will develop concentration and rhythmic freedom in a splendid way. The hands may be reversed: —

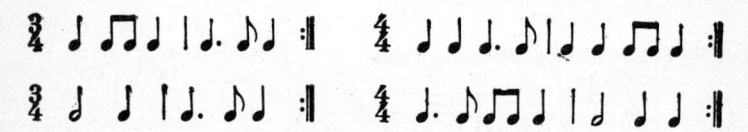

Harmonic: Use examples 24 and 25 as ear-training.

Verbal Dictation: Dictate some two-part exercises and then have the class sing them for sight-reading.

ASSIGNMENT

Keyboard Work: Commit to memory Ex. 24 (*a*), (*b*), (*c*), and (*d*), and be able to play them in several other keys. Make the slight changes needed and play them also in f minor.

Written Work: Harmonize the following:—

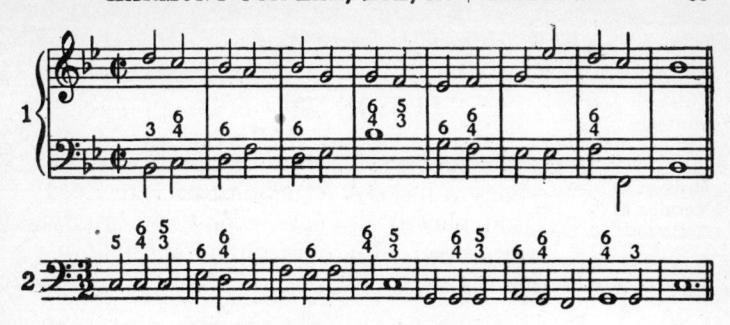

ADDITIONAL EXERCISES
(WRITTEN WORK)

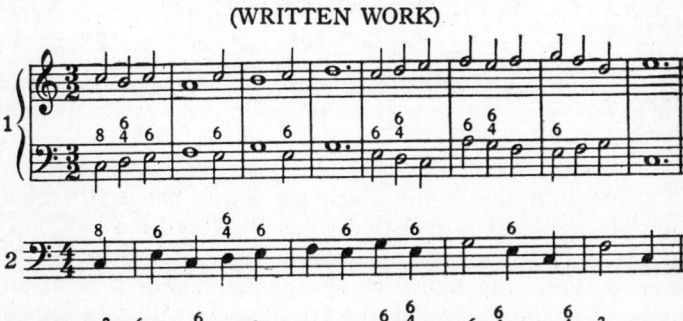

(EAR-TRAINING)

Verbal Dictation:—

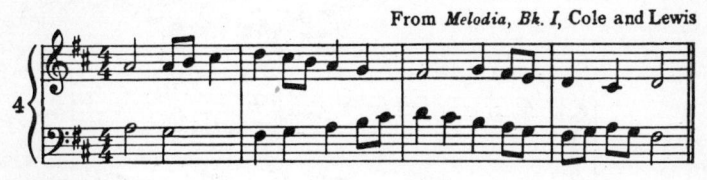

From *Melodia, Bk. I*, Cole and Lewis

Melodic:—

LESSON 23

Broken Chord Version of A Period

For the first step in using chords to accompany a melody, let us turn back to Ex. 19 and play it through (except the last two measures) with some one of the following figures in the right hand (a), (b), or (c):—

Note that the figure which we use is the length of a quarter-note and is repeated when the chord is a half-note in length. Because the rhythm is lively, it will be better here to keep the figure going through all four beats in measure 4, and to close in the 8th measure with two figures followed by a half-note chord.

Now write the melody itself on a third staff for voice, or violin, and you will have a simple but interesting use of our present vocabulary, beginning as follows:—

Ex. 26

SIGHT-SINGING AND EAR-TRAINING

Chromatic Scale: For sight-singing purposes the chromatic scale is usually notated as given below:—

[Musical notation: Beginning on C ascending — Do di Re ri Mi Fa fi So si La li Ti Do; descending — Do Ti te La le So se Fa Mi me Re ra Do]

[Musical notation: Beginning on E♭ (same syllables), ascending and descending]

Notice that the vowel *i* (pronounced e) is substituted in the syllable names for the ascending chromatics; and that *e* (pronounced ā) is substituted for the descending chromatics with the one exception — *a* (pronounced äh) on the second degree.

However, *fi* (♯4) and *te* (♭7) are sometimes used in both ascending and descending forms to replace *se* and *li*. *Se* is seldom used but *li* is frequently found in melodies.

Practice writing this scale according to the following plan:

1. Write the major scale of the given key in whole notes.
2. Mark the half-steps (3⌣4, 7⌣8) with a curved line.
3. Working from left to right, alter each possible degree — that is, where the curved line does not "lock the door"—using sharps ascending, flats descending. Use solid note-heads with no stems to indicate the chromatics.

Practice singing chromatic scales.[1]

---

[1] If a phonograph is available, look up the record "Hymn to John the Baptist" (770 A. D.) sung by Olive Kline. After a brief history of the syllable names, and the hymn, various scales are sung. It is worth while for the student to hear scales sung by a beautiful voice, to sing with the record and then alone. (The minor scales may be omitted until Lesson 30.)

68 HARMONY FOR EAR, EYE, AND KEYBOARD

ASSIGNMENT

Keyboard Work: Play a broken chord version of Ex. 20 while one of your classmates plays the melody an octave higher. Try it in this way in D or F.

Written Work: Complete Ex. 19 as begun in Ex. 26. Harmonize the following soprano, using four different kinds of six-four chords. Name them: —

ADDITIONAL EXERCISES
(WRITTEN WORK)

Six-fours: —

Passing Tones and Embellishments: —

IV – I – V

(EAR-TRAINING)

Tonal: —

Melodic: —

LESSON 24[1]

Ear-Training Review

The work will be based on the ear-training drill in Lessons 16 to 23. A wisely chosen list of short questions covering the points which the teacher considers most important should require about twenty minutes of the class hour, the remainder of the hour to be left for the keyboard review.

Keyboard Work Review

Proceed as in Lesson 15. The problems will be limited to those of the keyboard assignments in Lessons 16 to 23 inclusive, or, at the teacher's discretion, to new questions of the same kind and grade of difficulty.

Written Work Review

Nine problems in three groups. A lesson should contain at least one problem from each of these groups. Vocabulary: the primary triads and their inversions, also passing tones and the embellishment.

Group 1

Original eight-measure periods.

Write and harmonize, using the tonic six-four chord in a half cadence at the end of the first four measures and in a perfect authentic cadence at the close: —

[1] As in Lesson 15, two or three lessons might be devoted to this review lesson.

70 HARMONY FOR EAR, EYE, AND KEYBOARD

Group 2

Passing tones and embellishments.

Harmonize, number the chords, and indicate the ornaments:—

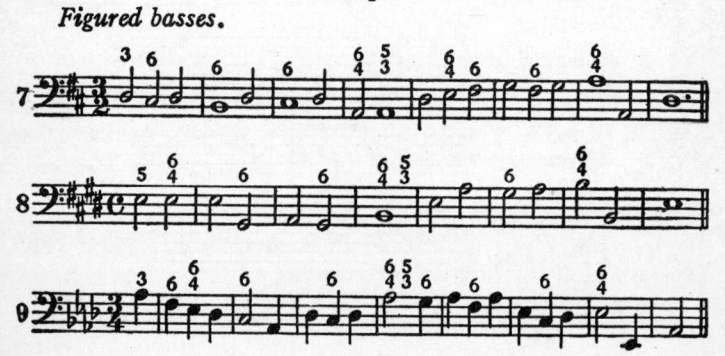

Group 3

Figured basses.

LESSON 25

Diminished and Augmented Intervals

We have seen (Lesson 10) how all perfect and major intervals can be readily measured by reckoning in the major scale from the lower note as a keynote, and also that any major interval becomes minor when reduced in size a chromatic half-step.

A *Diminished Interval* results when any perfect or minor interval is reduced in size a chromatic half-step. Read:—

Dim. 8   3   4   7   3   5   5   5   5

Diminished primes, seconds, and sixths do not occur in harmonic relations.[1]

An *Augmented Interval* results when any perfect or major interval is increased in size a chromatic half-step. Read:—

Aug. 4   4   2   2   8   6   4   6   5   2

Augmented thirds and sevenths do not occur in harmonic relations.[1]

A bird's-eye view of all the used intervals is afforded by the following chart. This should be memorized so that you can put it on the board from memory:—

[1] Highly chromatic music may contain these intervals. They certainly can be written, but in practice a diminished prime is inconceivable, and there are better ways to express what the others sound like.

HARMONY FOR EAR, EYE, AND KEYBOARD

Intervals
$\begin{cases} 1, 4, 5, 8, \\ \text{(Not dim. 1)} \\ 2, 6, \\ 3, 7, \end{cases}$
$\begin{cases} \text{Aug.} \\ \text{Per.} \\ \text{Dim.} \end{cases}$
$\begin{cases} \text{Aug.} \\ \text{Maj.} \\ \text{Min.} \end{cases}$
$\begin{cases} \text{Maj.} \\ \text{Min.} \\ \text{Dim.} \end{cases}$

A Model for the 23 used intervals reckoned from D.

P. P   A.P.   Mi. 2   Ma. 2   A. 2
Ma. 3 Mi. 3 D. 3   D. 4   P. 4 A. 4   D. 5 P. 5 A. 5
Mi. 6 Ma. 6 A. 6   Ma. 7   Mi. 7 D 7   D. 8 P. 8 A. 8

When inverted, diminished intervals become augmented and augmented intervals become diminished.

Intervals are divided into two classes: *consonant* and *dissonant*.

Consonant intervals are classed as *perfect* and *imperfect*.

The perfect consonances are the perfect prime, fifth, and octave.

The imperfect consonances are the major and minor thirds and sixths.

All other intervals are dissonant, including the perfect fourth, which, though theoretically consonant, because of its small ratio, is musically a discord, and, like all discords, requires resolution; i. e., progression to a consonance — an interval of repose.

EAR-TRAINING

Key and interval drill involving some chromatics. (See Lesson 16.)
Two-part Ear-Training: —

[musical notation with markings: A.4, D.5, A.2, D 5, D.5, A.4]

Notice the tendency of the augmented intervals to spread apart and of the diminished intervals to draw together.

Compare the sound of the following intervals. Although the first of each pair of intervals looks formidable, notice that the sound is almost without exception that of some familiar interval: —

[musical notation with markings: A.P., Mi.2, A.2, Mi.3, D.3, Ma.2, A.4, D.5, A.5, Mi.6, A.6, Mi.7, D.7, Ma.6, D.8, Ma.7]

ASSIGNMENT

Keyboard Work: Play and spell the 23 used intervals from G, D, and F♯.

Written Work: Following the model, write the 23 used intervals from E♭, A, and C♯. Be ready to put the interval chart on the board.

LESSON 26

The Dominant Seventh Chord
If we add another third above the dominant triad (minor seventh from the root), there results the *Dominant Seventh Chord*. This is our first and, by far, most important dissonant chord. It is the same in both major and minor (compare the following):—

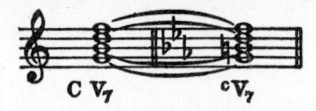

[musical notation: C V₇ and ᶜV₇]

Spell and play this chord (in one hand) in every key. To think it quickly, add a minor third to the top of a major triad.

With a figured bass, the dominant seventh chord is indicated by 7 (in minor $\frac{7}{\natural}$, $\frac{7}{\sharp}$) the other figures, as shown below, being understood, but rarely needed:—

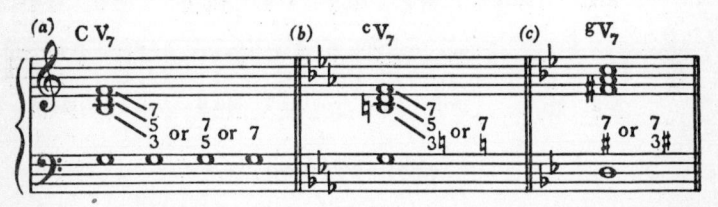

[musical notation: (a) C V₇ — 7/5/3 or 7/5 or 7; (b) ᶜV₇ — 7/5♭/3 or 7/♮; (c) ᵍV₇ — 7/♯ or 7/3♯]

The seventh is a dissonance and requires resolution (progression) down one degree to a consonance. The meaning of this term, *resolution*, and the reason for resolving a dissonance become apparent the moment we play a passage of music and end it with a dominant seventh chord. Imagine a choir ending an anthem in this way. Such a close is clearly impossible, and it is this demand of the ear for further progression to a consonance that proves this seventh to be a discord.

Rules for the Regular Resolution to the Tonic Triad

The regular resolution of the dominant seventh chord is to the tonic triad as follows: The root leaps up a fourth, or down a fifth; the seventh goes down a degree; the fifth usually goes down a degree, sometimes up a degree; the third (leading tone) goes up a degree, or, if in an inner voice, may leap down a third to the fifth of the tonic triad, as in Ex. 27 (a), (b), (c).

In Root Position Fifth Omitted

In root position the dominant seventh chord frequently omits its fifth and doubles the root. In this case the upper root is kept as a common tone and the succeeding tonic triad will be complete. [See (e) and (f).]

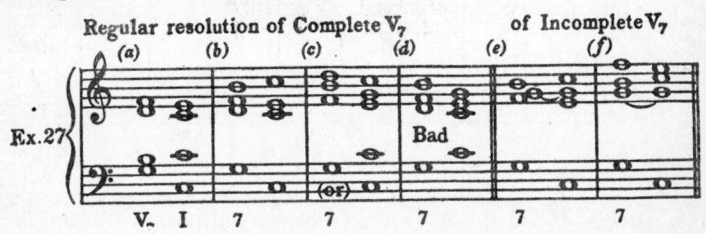

Ex. 27 — Regular resolution of Complete V$_7$ (a) (b) (c) (d) — of Incomplete V$_7$ (e) (f) — V$_7$ I 7 7 7 7 7 — Bad

Importance to the Composer

The dominant seventh chord is so important to the composer that he can scarcely write without it. With it we can now harmonize many folk-songs and other well known melodies that, thus far, we could not touch. Get thoroughly acquainted with this chord and it will prove to be one of your best friends. Play it and resolve it in every key. The models above (Ex. 27) are equally good in minor. Play a minor tonic triad in place of the major, but *keep the V^7 just as it is*, and you have changed all these to minor.

Introduction of the Seventh of the Dominant Seventh Chord

Although a dissonance, and formerly subjected to many rules, the seventh of the dominant seventh chord is now introduced almost as freely as the tones of a triad. If in the previous chord, the seventh is generally kept as a common tone, as in Ex. 28 (*a*); but one must avoid the parallel fifths at (*b*). When the seventh is not in the previous chord, its smoothest entry is stepwise from above, as at (*c*) or (*d*). Taken descending stepwise *from the root of its own triad*, as at (*d*), it is termed a *passing seventh*. Similar motion of all the voices, as at (*e*) and (*f*), can not be condemned — in fact, nearly any reasonable freedom is available to the student. The seventh may be added to its own triad by an upward leap, as at (*g*). *Do not leap in the same direction to both root and seventh (from another chord)*, as at (*h*).

Ex. 28

In Ex. 28 (*c*) the fifth in V⁷ between alto and soprano is diminished. These are therefore not bad parallels. At (*f*) the leap of an octave is equivalent to note-repetition. At (*h*) the seventh in outer voices is so exposed as to be very disagreeable.

SIGHT-SINGING AND EAR-TRAINING

Sight-Singing: Spend a few minutes on two-part sight-reading.

Two-part Ear-Training: When having occasion to write chromatics, be sure to analyze the tendency of the chromatic tone before notating it. If its tendency is upward, use the notation of the ascending form of the chromatic scale; similarly, if its tendency is downward, use the notation of the descending scale: —

Ex: *Mi* **ri** *mi*, not *Mi* **me** *mi*;
Re **ra** *do*, not *Re* **di** *do*.
So **fi** *fa* is the common exception to this rule.

Harmonic: Use examples 27(a), (e), and other positions of V⁷.

ASSIGNMENT

Keyboard Work: Play (and spell) the V⁷ in one hand in every key. Play and resolve the V⁷ to I in every major and minor key. In some of these omit the fifth and double the root in the V⁷. Sometimes place the fifth highest, again the third, etc.

Written Work: Harmonize the following:—

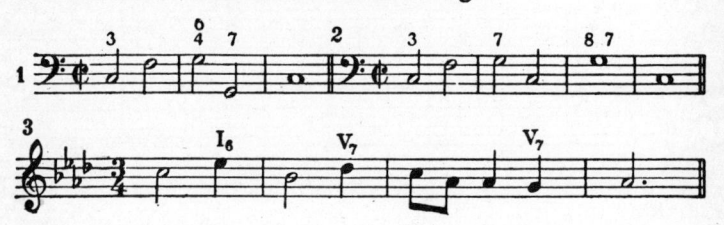

ADDITIONAL EXERCISES

(WRITTEN WORK)

LESSON 27

Inversions of the Dominant Seventh Chord

The dominant seventh chord has three inversions whose regular resolution is to the tonic triad, as before. Lead its seventh down a degree, likewise its fifth, tie the root as a common tone, and lead the third up a degree. *All four tones must now be used.* Reckon up from the bass and you will see, in each case, the meaning of the figures, which are used in full only where necessary. Notice that the V^2 must resolve to a first inversion; also, that if the fifth of V^2 is in the soprano, it may leap up a fourth, as in Ex. 29 (*b*). Memorize Ex. 29 (*a*). It contains, in a nutshell, the V^7 and all its inversions.

Ex. 29

One position or inversion may follow another provided the last form resolves, as in Ex. 30(*a*); one exception — *do not write* V^2—V^7. The bass in V^2 insists on downward movement (*b*).

Doubled Third

A I^6 with doubled third may connect V_3^4 with V^2. No voice leaps. This doubled third is like a passing tone and, as such, is not too prominent (*c*).

A V_3^4—I^6 is good with both seventh and fifth ascending a degree (*d*). Here the ear is satisfied because the bass has taken the note (usually lower octave) to which the seventh would have gone. Again, these are not bad parallels; the fifth in V_3^4 is dimished.

HARMONY FOR EAR, EYE, AND KEYBOARD   79

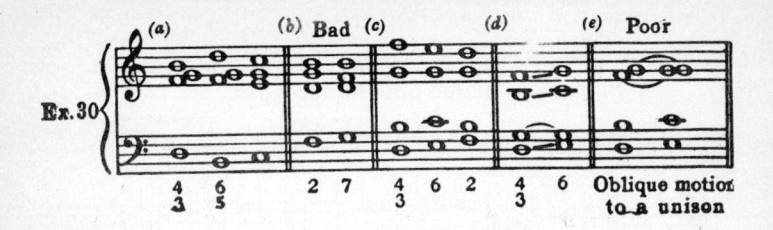

Ex. 30

(a)   (b) Bad (c)   (d)   (e) Poor

$\begin{smallmatrix}4\\3\end{smallmatrix}$ $\begin{smallmatrix}6\\5\end{smallmatrix}$ 2 7 $\begin{smallmatrix}4\\3\end{smallmatrix}$ 6 2 $\begin{smallmatrix}4\\3\end{smallmatrix}$ 6   Oblique motion to a unison

EAR-TRAINING

Melodic:—

Harmonic: Use the following examples and other arrangements. Listen closely to the bass note.   Although V_3^4 and V^2 resolve downward, V^2 goes to I^6 and is therefore easily recognized: —

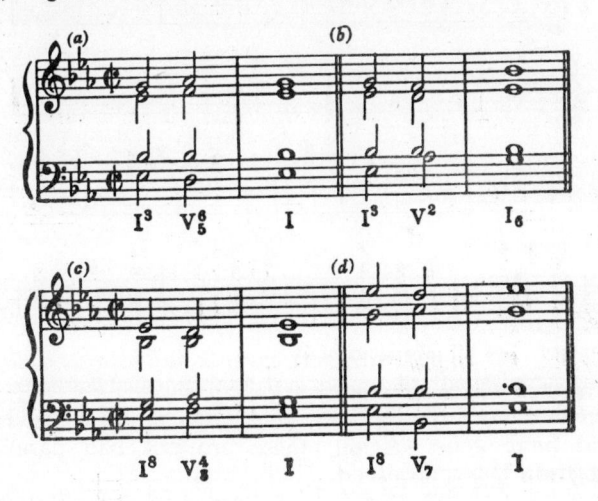

(a)   (b)

I^3 V_5^6 I I^3 V^2 I_6

(c)   (d)

I^3 V_3^4 I I^3 V_7 I

ASSIGNMENT

Keyboard Work: Play and resolve the inversions of V⁷ to I in several major and minor keys.

Written Work:—

ADDITIONAL EXERCISES

(WRITTEN WORK)

A Double chant

Unfigured. Use all inversions of V_7:—

LESSON 28

All the Triads In addition to the major and minor triads, music contains two others: diminished and augmented.

A *Diminished Triad* contains a minor third and a *diminished fifth* (the sign °).

An *Augmented Triad* contains a major third and an augmented fifth (the sign ′).

If we examine the two scales of triads which follow and give each the correct set of numerals, we shall get the following:—

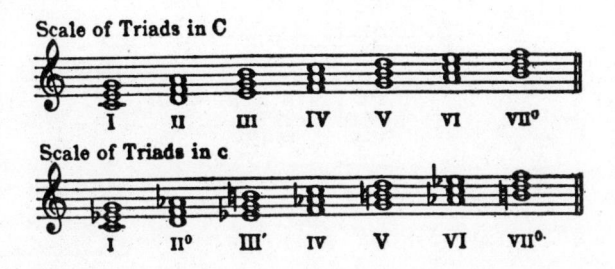

Scale of Triads in C

I II III IV V VI VII°

Scale of Triads in c

I II° III′ IV V VI VII°

Notice that we build in minor from the harmonic minor scale.

A table of the kinds of triads in each key may be written as follows:

Triads in Major			Triads in Minor			
Maj.	Min.	Dim.	Maj.	Min.	Dim.	Aug.
I	II	VII°	V	I	II°	III′
IV	III		VI	IV	VII°	
V	VI					

Memorize the above tables; in writing them be sure to contrast strongly the sizes of the numerals and to use the special signs as needed.

To Locate Triads To locate the triads in all the major keys in which they are found, proceed as follows:

Begin with the major triad C-E-G. Since there are three major triads in any major key (I, IV, V), this triad can be found where its root is I, — that is, in C; where its root is IV, — that is, in G; and where its root is V, — that is, in F. If this is not perfectly clear, write these three scales.

To locate a minor triad in major keys you must find the three keys where its root is in turn II, III, VI, of the scale. The diminished triad is easy to locate because it is on VII° only.

Triad table of a major, minor, and diminished triad on C, with all the major keys in which they can be found.

Ex. 31

Maj.	Min.	Dim.
I C	II B♭	VII° D♭
IV G	III A♭	
V F	VI E♭	

SIGHT-SINGING AND EAR-TRAINING

Melodic: Just as soon as possible, the pupil should get away from listening to music note by note and hear it phrase by phrase; just as, when reading literature, he grasps the thought of a long phrase, or often a whole sentence, instead of each separate word. One of the best means of developing this ability to think music in phrases is to sing original answers to a given phrase.

From time to time attention has been called to the period construction of the various melodies used for sight-singing and ear-training. We have noted the use of repetition — either tonal or rhythmic, or both — of sequence, of balance, of sufficient contrasting material to avoid monotony.

Below are two opening phrases of eight-measure melodies. Complete these melodies in several ways by singing answers to the apparent questions:—

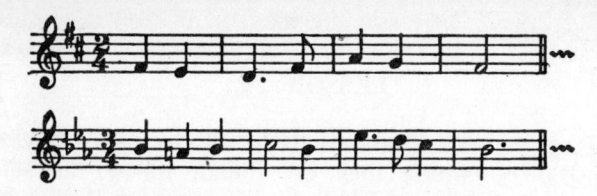

Drill on the chromatic scale, both singing and writing.

ASSIGNMENT

Keyboard Work: Play and spell all four kinds of triads on every white key.

Written Work: Write the triad table, Ex. 31, with A as the root of each of the three triads. Do the same with F♯ and B♭. Be prepared to put such a table on the board.

ADDITIONAL EXERCISES

(ORAL WORK)

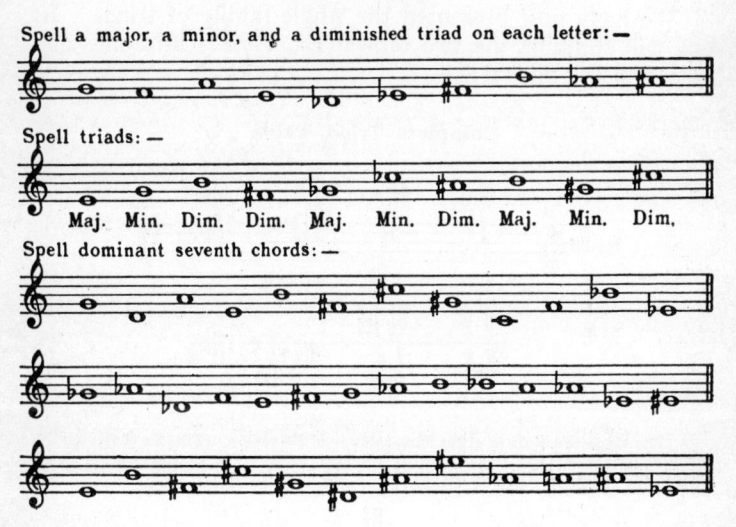

Spell a major, a minor, and a diminished triad on each letter:—

Spell triads:—

Maj. Min. Dim. Dim. Maj. Min. Dim. Maj. Min. Dim.

Spell dominant seventh chords:—

LESSON 29

All the Triads (Concluded)

To locate triads in all the minor keys in which they are found, follow the same general plan, as before (Lesson 28), but observe that, since there are but two major triads in a minor key (V, VI), our triad C-E-G can be found in but two minor keys; that is, where its root is V (scale of f), and where its root is VI (scale of e). Proceeding, you will locate a minor triad on I and IV, a diminished, on II° and VII°; and an augmented, on III′.

Triad table of all four triads on C with all the minor keys in which they can be found:—

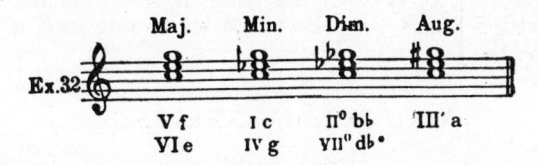

Ex. 32.

Maj.	Min.	Dim.	Aug.
V f	I c	II° b♭	III′ a
VI e	IV g	VII° d♭	

We have now presented the whole family of triads. If you will combine the two tables (Ex. 31, 32) into one, the following will appear:—

Complete Triad Table

Ex. 33.

Maj.	Min.	Dim.	Aug.
I C	II B♭	VII° D♭	
IV G	III A♭		
V F	VI E♭		
V f	I c	II° b♭	III′ a
VI e	IV g	VII° d♭[1]	

[1] The signature of d♭ is eight flats, relative of F♭ major. This is theoretically possible, but, in practice, one can avoid too large a signature by writing the same pitches and using sharps instead of flats: e. g., here c-e♭-g♭ sounds the same as b♯-d♯-f♯ in c♯ minor. This, however, is not intended to alter our table.

Draw a light line just below the major keys, keep all minor keys below the line, and you will not confuse the two halves of the table.

When you can put such a complete table on the board, reckoned from any letter, and keep all the contrasts and little signs just where they belong, you have made splendid progress in the mastery of many important details.

An excellent oral recitation in triad location is as follows (reading, for example, column one in Ex. 33):—

A major triad on C is C-E-G; it is found on one in the key of C, on four in G, on five in F; and in the minor keys it is on five in f, and on six in e.

In this way, some of you may spell the triad indicated on each of the following letters and locate it in all its keys, while others may go to the board and write the complete triad table.

Maj. Min. Dim. Aug. Maj. Dim. Aug. Dim. Maj.

Min. Dim. Aug. Dim. Maj. Min. Aug. Min. Dim.

EAR-TRAINING

Devote a few minutes to some one important drill selected from Lesson 25, on.

ASSIGNMENT

Keyboard Work: Play and spell all four kinds of triads on any letter #, ♭ or ♮.

Written Work: Write the scale of triads in a, e, and f, marking every triad with its proper number (and sign where needed). Write the triad table, Ex. 32, with G as the root of each of the four triads.
Write the complete triad table, Ex. 33, with E as the root of each chord. Do the same with D.

LESSON 30

The Secondary Triads in Major — The secondary triads are those formed on the second, third, and sixth degrees of the scale, in both major and minor. They are subordinate in character. Each of them is a kind of relative to the primary triad built on its third. This third is, in each case, one of the principal tones of the key and is more freely doubled than the third of any primary triad. In this lesson there will be no occasion to double the third.

The same general relationship exists in minor.

With a figured bass in the major key we can apply our general rules for contrary motion, and the common tone, and use these secondary triads almost as easily as we do the primary triads, with one important exception, as follows:—

Rule for II to V — **In the progression from II to V give up the common tone and lead the upper three voices in contrary motion to an ascending bass, to the nearest chord tones, as in Ex. 34(a), (b).** (Notice that this is treated as we treat IV to V, for which it is a substitute.)

Covered Octaves — From II to V the similar motion to the octave at 34 (*c*) is very unpleasant, and but little better in an inner voice (*d*). Our ears seem to accept this F in the II as a subdominant, a *down-tendency* tone. If it goes up we get our *first bad covered octaves*. When two voices go in similar motion (not parallel) to an octave, the progression is called *Covered Octaves*, or Hidden Octaves.

Covered Fifths — When two voices go in similar motion to a fifth, the progression is called *Covered Fifths*.

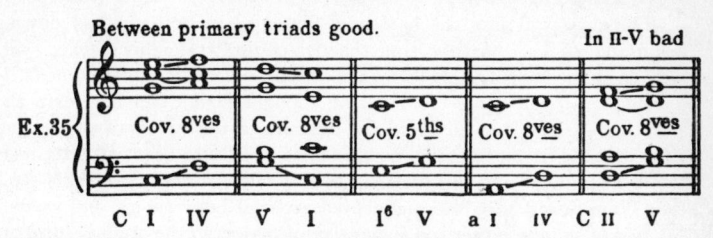

Between Primary Triads — Covered octaves and fifths make us no trouble between primary triads. The general rule for these is as follows:—

Between primary triads covered octaves are permitted if the lower voice leaps from root to root a fourth or a fifth, and the upper voice moves one degree; and *any* covered fifths are permitted if the upper voice moves one degree. You have been writing these constantly. They are good and so are many others the details of which we cannot discuss here. For the present keep your rule for II to V, and seek musical solutions just as you have been doing.

EAR-TRAINING

Minor: The teacher will play the above melody twice while the class listens. The third time the class will sing the syllables of the melody with the piano. (Books closed.)

Note the shifting of the key center from *do* in the first half to *la* in the second half. The minor mode, or scale material, simply means a grouping of the scale tones about **la** as a key center instead of about *do* as in major.

It is well to recall that, when studying the harmonic minor scale, it was found necessary to have a raised seventh in order to satisfy a natural inner craving for a leading tone. Therefore the syllables for this scale are: *La ti do re mi fa* **si** *la.*

The class will sing the harmonic minor scale, both up and down, beginning on C. As they sing the descending scale the teacher will play *fa*, that they may appreciate the difficulty of singing this augmented second, *si—fa*, in tune. *Fa* must be thought high. One can learn to sing this interval, but to avoid the difficulty a third form of the minor scale which is better for vocal purposes has come into use. It is termed the *melodic form*. In this scale six is also raised a chromatic half-step, thus doing away with the augmented interval between six and seven. *Mi fi si la* sounds rather too suggestive of major, so the original form of the scale is retained in descending. The following is therefore the pattern of the melodic minor scale: —

1—2⌒3—4—5—6—7⌒8—7—6⌒5—4—3⌒2—1
La ti⌣do re mi fi si⌣la so fa⌣mi re do⌣ti la.

Sing several melodic minor scales. Also sing the tonic chord (*la do mi la mi do la*) *repeatedly* until able easily to think *la* as the keynote.

The teacher will now play simple groups of tones in minor and the class will sing with the syllables, after one hearing.

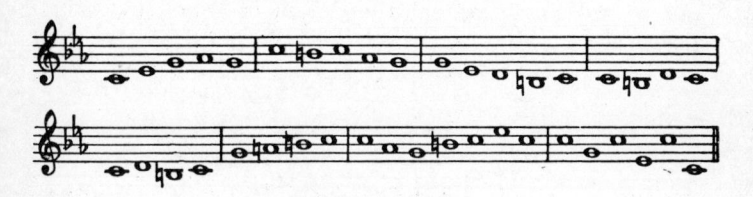

ASSIGNMENT

Keyboard Work: Play and transpose to several other major keys. Listen especially to V-vi and ii-V: —

HARMONY FOR EAR, EYE, AND KEYBOARD 89

Written Work: Harmonize. (Remember that a bass note with no figure is a root.):—

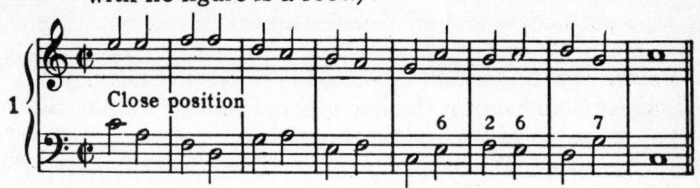

ADDITIONAL EXERCISES
(WRITTEN WORK)

Use V$_7$ in all inversions and use II – V at the close.

LESSON 31

Secondary Triads In Major (Con.) The most useful of the secondary triads is the supertonic in the form of II or II^6, used as a substitute for IV in various forms of half and full cadences. Its third is often doubled when in root position, and best doubled in first inversion. The rule for II to V does not apply to II-V^6, nor to V^7 in any form. We come now to such an increase in the possibilities that it is impossible to exhaust them within our limits. Study the following at the piano and by ear:—

In half cadence   Full cadences

The position of II with the fifth in the soprano is rather poor; hence, as a rule, we avoid this position if possible. But sometimes the preceding chord is such that this poor position of II is at least strongly invited and if used when the following triad is I$^6_4$ we get bad parallel fifths, as in Ex. 36 (*a*). In such a case, one should give up common tones and use contrary motion to the II (*b*). Sometimes open position of the II makes the same trouble (*c*).

Rule for II or II^6 to I$^6_4$ From II or II^6 to I$^6_4$ use contrary motion to an ascending bass to the nearest chord tones and do not have the fifths of the chords above the roots. (See Ex. 36).

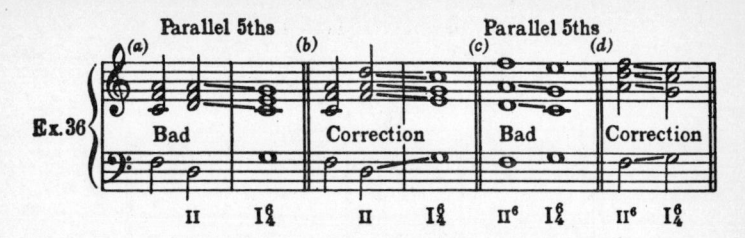

Ex. 36 [musical example showing Parallel 5ths (a) Bad, (b) Correction, (c) Bad, (d) Correction; with figures II, I⅔, II, I⅔, II⁶, I⅔, II⁶, I⅔]

Deceptive Cadence The VI with doubled third is next in value. It *precedes* V in the half cadence and *follows* V (or V⁷) in a new one, the *Deceptive Cadence*. You will see that this VI has tonic function and, having that, its third (tonic) is fine doubled. Listen to these in Ex. 37. The V⁷ should be complete when it precedes VI. See (*b*).

Ex. 37 [musical example with (a), (b), (c), (d)]

The VI in half cadence. The Deceptive Cadence (3 approaches.)

SIGHT-SINGING AND EAR-TRAINING

Scale Drill: Write the melodic minor scale beginning on C♯ and on F. Sing several minor scales and the tonic chord.

Verbal Dictation: Whole-notes in minor.

Tonal: Groups in minor similar to those given in the last lesson.

Melodic: The teacher will play very simple minor melodies for the class to sing and then write: —

[musical examples]

ASSIGNMENT

Keyboard Work: Play the following in several major keys:—

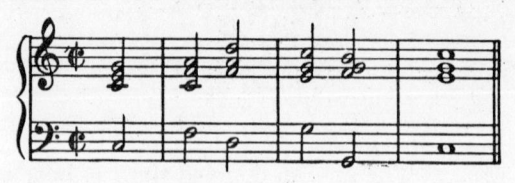

Written Work: Harmonize:—

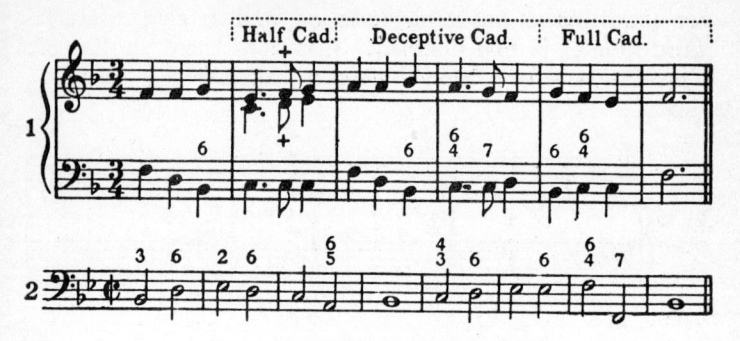

ADDITIONAL EXERCISES
(WRITTEN WORK)

LESSON 32

Secondary Triads in Minor   We shall limit our use of the secondary triads in minor to the supertonic and the submediant. The III' with its augmented fifth is better omitted in elementary work.

The supertonic triad in first inversion is used just as in major, but in root position its diminished fifth appears between the bass and an upper part and therefore the chord is poor. No diminished triad sounds well in root position. [(Ex. 38 (a).]

Augmented Second   The rules for II⁰, or II⁰⁶, to I⁶₄ and to V are the same here as in major (pp. 86, 90) and, in the case of II⁰-V, even more imperative; for now, if we keep the common tone, a new fault appears — the unvocal *augmented second* (b). *In diatonic harmony no voice is permitted to progress an augmented interval.*

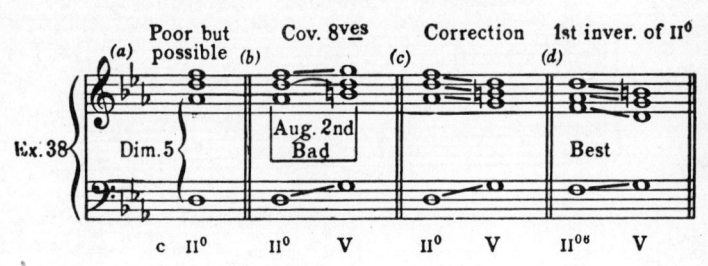

Ex. 38

The submediant is best in root position. When following or preceding the dominant, it requires a special rule to avoid the augmented second.

V-VI or VI-V in Minor   In the progression V-VI or VI-V always double the third in VI and do not omit the fifth. Two voices move contrary to the bass. [See Ex. 39(a), (b), (c).]

When VI has a doubled third its connection with other chords requires care to avoid overlapping.

94 HARMONY FOR EAR, EYE, AND KEYBOARD

Overlapping   *Overlapping* occurs, when, for example, the tenor in one chord is higher than the alto in the preceding chord. In this and similar cases the voices overlap, or encroach upon each other's territory. This is bad [(d), (e)].

One form of overlapping is permitted. This is when tenor and bass go to, or from, a unison between I-IV, IV-I, or I-V, V-I (f).

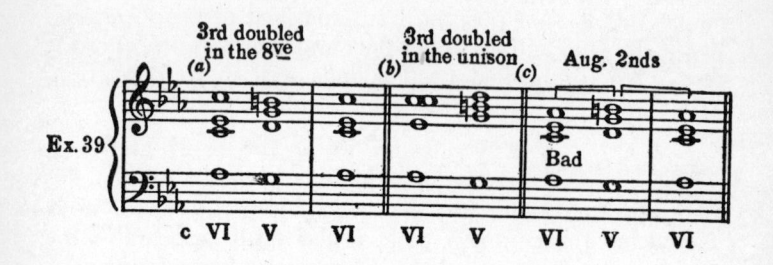

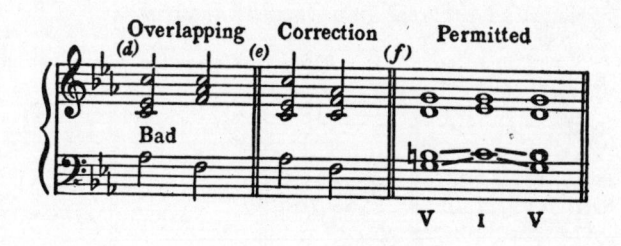

Ex. 39

SIGHT-SINGING AND EAR-TRAINING

Sight-Singing: If no minor material can be placed in the students' hands, the teacher can copy a half dozen minor melodies on the board for the class to sing at sight.

Singing Answers: Use these opening phrases as ear-training. The class will complete them in several ways.

HARMONY FOR EAR, EYE, AND KEYBOARD 95

Harmonic: The teacher will play I V⁷ I and I V⁷ VI for comparison, in both major and minor, and in several positions, as ear work. Notice that in minor VI is a major triad, whereas in major it is a minor triad.

ASSIGNMENT

Keyboard Work: Play in several minor keys:—

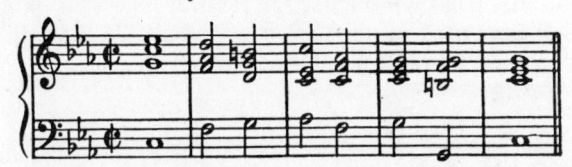

Written Work: Harmonize. In a melody, except where a chord is indicated, choose any material within your vocabulary:—

LESSON 33

The Triad on the Leading Tone — The leading tone triad is an incomplete dominant seventh chord (a V^7 without its root) and its treatment is largely determined from this fact. It is dependent. Its diminished fifth (original seventh) is dissonant and requires careful treatment. The fifth must move stepwise (i. e., without a leap) to the next chord, but is freer in two respects, — it may move up or down, and it may be doubled. If doubled, the two fifths resolve in contrary motion. The root (leading tone) must not be doubled and must move up a half-step to the keynote. The third, being consonant with each of the other tones, is freely doubled (this is best) and may progress by a leap, but seldom does so. In these lessons this triad will be used in its first inversion only.

Our best uses of the chord are shown in Example 40, which should be played and analyzed:—

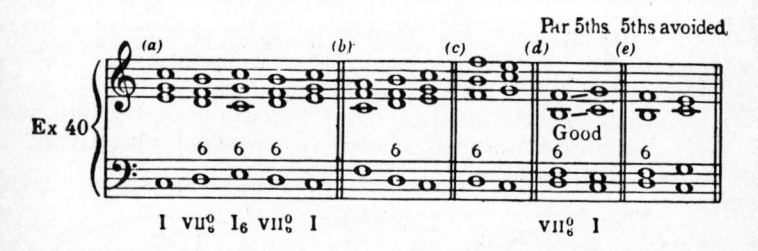

Ex 40

(a) (b) (c) (d) Par 5ths. 5ths avoided. (e)

  6 6 6   6   6   Good 6   6

I vii°₆ I₆ vii°₆ I   vii°₆ I

Consecutive Chords of the Sixth — When the bass leaps from the third of one chord to the third of another, one doubles the root or the fifth in whatever affords the best soprano, as in Ex. 41(a).

With a stepwise bass it is often better to double the third in one of the triads rather than avoid it at the cost of making the passage too thin. For example, (b) is certainly better than (c), which sounds like three parts only. When three successive sixths with a stepwise bass in *one direction* are required, one may, if the bass ascends, use close position and double in turn the 5th, the 3rd, and the root; or if it descends, double the root, the 3rd, and the 5th. In these cases no voice needs to leap, as in Ex. 41(*d*). It would be well to transpose all the following to other keys:—

EAR-TRAINING

Harmonic: Use Ex. 29, the class writing soprano, bass, and chord numerals. The teacher will transpose this to c minor, at the piano. What changes of notation are now necessary?

Use an exercise in minor similar to the one given below. Have the class sing the syllables of the soprano and of the bass, as they write each part. Complete with the chord numerals in the usual way: —

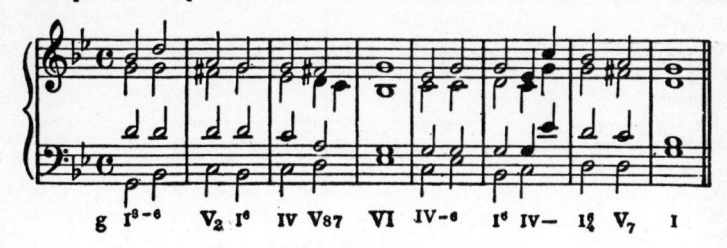

ASSIGNMENT

Keyboard Work: Transpose to several major keys:—

98 HARMONY FOR EAR, EYE, AND KEYBOARD

Written Work: Harmonize. In No. 2 each note with a (+) is the root of a triad in first inversion:—

ADDITIONAL EXERCISES
(WRITTEN WORK)

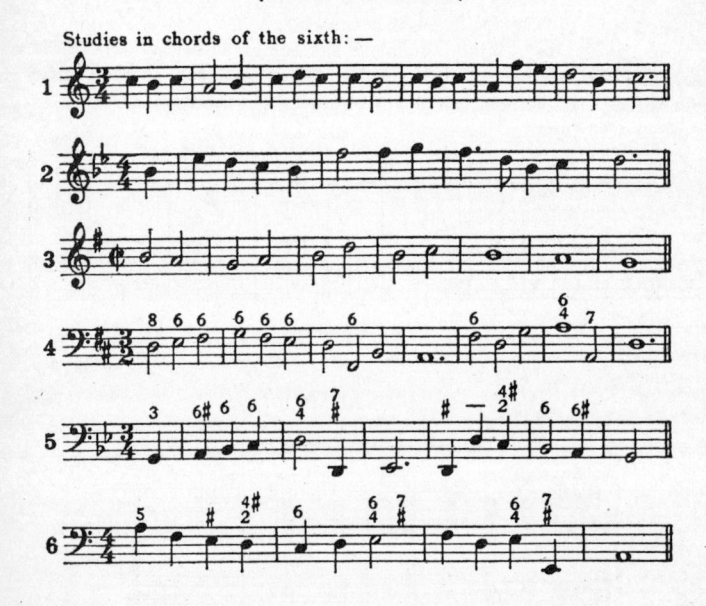

Studies in chords of the sixth:—

LESSON 34

Rules and Exceptions If you have been a bit distressed by the number of new problems which have come in with the secondary triads, no one can blame you. An increased vocabulary does, indeed, bring its troubles; but these soon vanish and your increased resources become a satisfaction. Our rules, too, are not so numerous as you would think at first — about a dozen thus far, which serve to counsel us and afford a basis of judgment in all special cases. Exceptions to the general rules are numerous. Harmony must admit the truth of this accusation, but it does so without apology, for no art grows without change. The obsolete will be discarded and some exceptions will become new rules, but in the meantime we must conserve the fine gold of Beethoven, while standing ready to accept "real nuggets" from the moderns. The beginner must establish a solid general basis. Before he has done this he wastes his time if he attempts to experiment with "special effects" dreamed over at the keyboard.

Similar Motion of All Four Voices Similar motion of all the voices and the resulting covered octaves and fifths, while seldom necessary, may sometimes afford a positive gain to the melodic line of the soprano, or to the position of the harmony.

From II to V In the progression from II-V the downward tendency of the upper three voices is so strong that they had better descend even with a descending bass, as in Ex. 42(a):—

Ex. 42

(a) Good   (b) The same bass — A poor soprano

In Ex. 42(a), covered fifths in the soprano and bass appear with both parts leaping. This is good here, but we must limit such fifths to this particular progression from II to V. Here they sound well for some very good reasons, too detailed for this place.

From I or I⁶ to II₆ In the progression from I or I⁶ with doubled root, to II⁶ with doubled third, all four parts may go up, if the roots are above the fifths; or down, if the soprano takes 3-2 in the scale, as in 43(a), (b), (c). In each of these cases, the II⁶ functions as a subdominant chord and the covered octaves to F are not to be condemned.

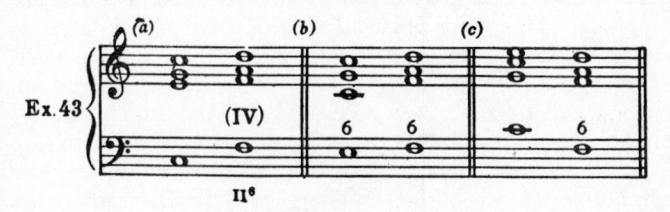

Leading Tone Not Doubled The progression IV⁶-V⁶, with roots in the soprano, affords a pleasing idiom; but the student is warned to think of this as a rather special case, because the third of V⁶ is the leading tone and must not be doubled. This is not an exception to the procedure in last lesson but a place where you cannot choose which third you will double. [See Ex. 44(a), (b).] But in this progression you can avoid doubling the third in both chords; nothing, however, is gained by it (c).

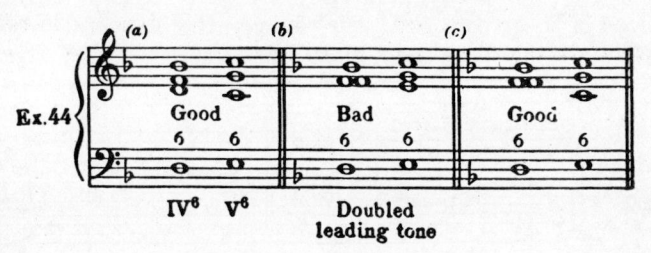

SIGHT-SINGING AND EAR-TRAINING

Sight-Singing: Have the class sing each of the three lower parts of "Sweet and Low," and then the four parts unaccompanied.

Tonal: Groups of tones involving chromatics:—

ASSIGNMENT

Keyboard Work: Play in several major keys:—

Written Work: Harmonize:—
Supply the missing soprano.

1

One or two chords of the sixth in every measure.

2   IV⁶ V⁶   II⁶ V

LESSON 35

The Supertonic Seventh Chord The secondary seventh chords are those built on the secondary triads. The most important secondary seventh is that on the supertonic, and is the only one of these which we shall use till near the close of these lessons.

The *Supertonic Seventh Chord* is obtained by adding another third above the supertonic triad. This added tone is a minor seventh from the root and, like the dominant seventh, a mild dissonance requiring resolution.

Cadencing Resolution Just as the dominant seventh chord goes to the tonic; i. e., to a chord whose root is a perfect fifth lower (or fourth higher), called the *Cadencing Resolution*; so this supertonic seventh chord finds its normal progression to be the cadencing resolution to V or V^7. Notice that in the cadencing resolution, with root positions, as in Ex. 45(c), the fifth must be omitted and the root doubled in alternate seventh chords, the third of one chord becoming the seventh in the next. The relation of the roots, the chords, and their practical use may be shown as follows:—

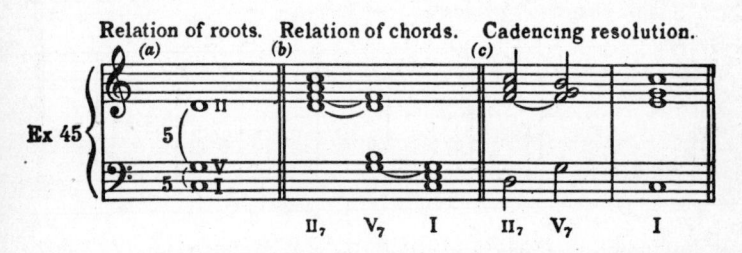

The behavior of this chord is so similar to that of the dominant seventh that its treatment needs very few rules. It is finest in its first inversion but may be used in root position and in any inversion. When inverted, omit no tone.

HARMONY FOR EAR, EYE, AND KEYBOARD

Strict Usage in First Lessons The following very conservative rules should be mastered by the beginner. Preparation and resolution are factors in harmony which challenge the treatment of every discord. Much of the charm in modern music arises from not preparing the discords, and when not resolved they may be said to "evaporate."[1]

While recognizing the splendid possibilities opened to music in this alluring and unfettered field, we must urge you strongly, in these first lessons, strictly to observe the rules. You can build best on this foundation.

Rules for the Supertonic Seventh Chord 1. *Prepare the seventh*, that is, have it in the preceding chord in the same voice (direct preparation), as in Ex. 46 (*a*); or in the preceding chord in some other voice (preparation by substitution), as in (*b*); or it may enter freely as a passing seventh (*c*).

2. *Resolve the seventh* down a degree (active resolution), as in Ex. 46 (*a*); or, if it is in the next chord, keep it as a common tone (passive resolution), as in (*d*). The six-four chord in (*d*) may be considered an interpolation, the real resolution to the dominant being delayed.

EAR-TRAINING

Melodic: Melodies involving chromatics and 6-8 measure. Think 6-8 as a combination of two triplets. Given the same tempo, 6/8 ♩. ♩. | ♫♩. | sounds exactly like 2/4 ♩ ♩ | ♫♩ |

A. Eaglefield Hull, *Modern Harmony,* pp 83, 111.

Or this may be written in 2-4 with triplets.

ASSIGNMENT

Keyboard Work: Play and transpose the following to several minor keys. These are typical cadence formulas and equally good in either mode:—

II$^{o6}_{5}$ V$_{87}$ II$^{o6}_{5}$ I$^{6}_{4}$ V$_7$

Written Work: In the first of these supply the inner parts, and in the second use two II$^{o6}_{5}$ chords:—

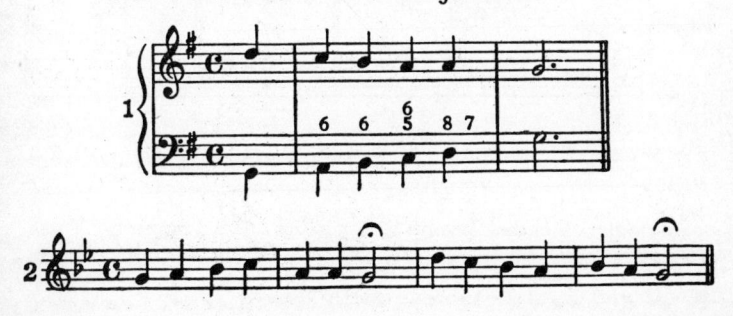

LESSON 36

The Sequence — A *Sequence* is a succession of similar melodic or harmonic progressions, ascending or descending in some symmetrical fashion.

A Harmonic Sequence

Ex. 47

Design Repeated — In Ex. 47 the first measure is the design or pattern. The chords in this pattern are connected in the regular way. The tenor has the common tone and keeps it; the soprano moves from the third in the first chord to the fifth in the next; and, in each repetition of the design, the tenor must keep the common tone and the soprano go from third to fifth as before. In this manner each voice gets its cue from what it did in the design.

Sequence Justifies Licenses — A sequence justifies several otherwise questionable progressions: for example, in this model (1) the common tone is given up in reaching the first chord of the repetition, (2) the triad on the leading tone is used in root position and its root is doubled, and (3) the bass leaps an augmented fourth from the third to the fourth bar. All of these points are quite subordinate to the plan as a whole and hence are ignored. The procedure described will vary according to the design. No two sequences are likely to require the same treatment. It may be added that covered octaves and fifths — *but not parallels* — and similar motion of all the parts are permitted if the sequence demands them.

The design may contain more or less than a measure. It does not necessarily begin with the first measure. This must be determined from the character of the given part.

SIGHT-SINGING AND EAR-TRAINING

Melodic:—

Complete a four or eight measure melody, making use of the sequence.

Use the following melody as ear-training. Then sketch an accompaniment in. ♩ ♩ Mark all ornamental tones: —

Sight-Singing: Selection chosen for its illustrative character — chromatics, 6-8 rhythm, the sequence, etc.

ASSIGNMENT

Keyboard Work: Transpose the following sequence to other major keys:—

Written Work: Add the missing parts. The portions of an exercise not truly sequential enjoy no special relaxation of the rules:—

ADDITIONAL EXERCISES
(WRITTEN WORK)

LESSON 37

Ear-Training Review — The work will be based on the ear-training drill from lesson 25 to this point. The choice of this list of questions must be left to the teacher.

Keyboard Work Review — The lessons from 25 to 36 afford keyboard work that is very important. The review should lay special emphasis upon the dominant seventh chord with its resolution (including its inversions) and on spelling and playing any chord or interval used thus far.

Written Work Review — Ten problems in three groups. A lesson should contain at least one problem from each of these groups.

Group 1

Intervals, chords, chord tables, resolutions, etc:—

1. Write the 23 used intervals reckoned from F#. Also be ready to put the interval chart on the board from memory.

2. Write the scale of triads in g# and Bb, marking every triad with its proper number (and sign where needed). Also write the complete triad table with C# as the root of each of the four triads.

3. Write the dominant seventh chord in root position and all its inversions, with resolution, in the key of Ab. Figure each. Do the same in g# and F#.

4. Give the key, figuring, and resolution of each of the following:—

HARMONY FOR EAR, EYE, AND KEYBOARD 109

LESSON 38

Modulation Modulation by the Dominant Seventh Chord to the Dominant and the Subdominant Keys in Major.

Modulation is the process of changing, in the course of a piece of music, from one key to another.

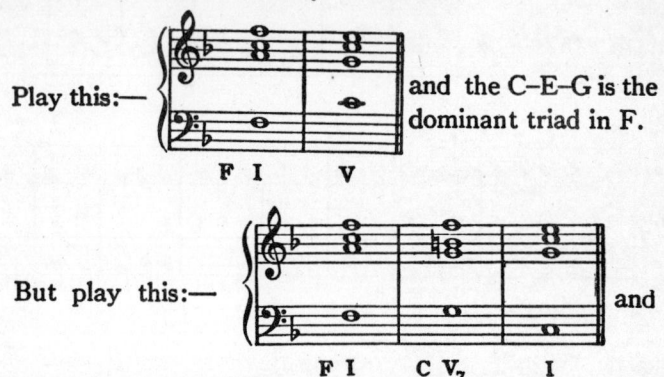

Play this:— [musical example: F I V] and the C–E–G is the dominant triad in F.

But play this:— [musical example: F I C V₇ I] and C–E–G has been defined as a tonic triad in C.

Dominant Seventh Defines the Key For no major key except C contains the chord G–B–D–F. We know that all the sharp keys contain F♯, and all the flat keys B♭. There remains, then, to add a cadence to confirm or establish this new tonic chord. The simplest and strongest cadence for our purpose is one we already know, the IV (or II⁶ or II⁶₅) I⁶₄ V⁷ I formula. The modulation complete stands thus:—

Ex. 48

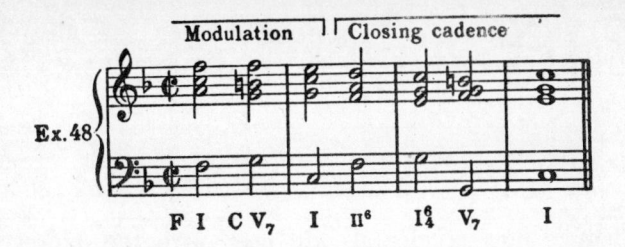

F I C V₇ I II⁶ I⁶₄ V₇ I

Or suppose we were in the key of G, as for example in the following:—

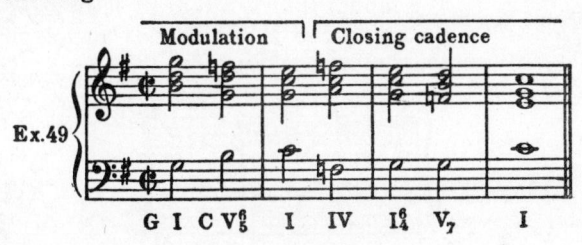

Ex. 49

G I C V⁶₅ I IV I⁶₄ V₇ I

Cadence to Establish New Key Our problem is to reach the new dominant seventh in any form we choose and through its resolution to define the new tonic, then to establish it. The two models given above (48 and 49) should be committed to memory and transposed, at first to a few keys and later to every key. But it would be a very bad mistake to allow this to become a matter of finger memory only. In every key, be awake mentally to each step of the proceeding. Notice that, in the first model, you modulate to the key a perfect fifth higher; i. e., to the dominant key: while, in the other, you modulate to the subdominant key. These will make good board work also.

Any inversion of the dominant seventh is good for these modulations. Ex. 48 may equally well begin in the following three ways:—

112 HARMONY FOR EAR, EYE, AND KEYBOARD

Notice how accidentals are used with the figures to indicate the (♯) or (♮) not in the signature. A figured bass that modulates, frequently requires many such.

Augmented Fourth Unvocal We cannot do Ex. 50 (c) by letting the bass go up to the B for that is an augmented fourth, unvocal and forbidden:—

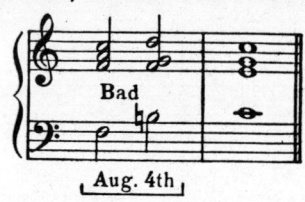

SIGHT-SINGING AND EAR-TRAINING

Sight Singing: Sing the four parts of "Santa Lucia," as in previous lessons. Have the class write from memory as much of the bass part of the refrain as they can. The teacher will then play the refrain once, emphasizing the bass, and the class will correct and complete their solution by ear.

Melodic: Bass Staff:—

ASSIGNMENT

Keyboard Work: Modulate, using Ex. 48 as a model, from C–G, G–D, D–A, B♭–F, E♭–B♭.
Modulate, using Ex. 49 as a model, from C–F, F–B♭, B♭–E♭, G–C, A–D.

Written Work: Harmonize, indicating carefully with the key letters and proper chord numerals the part in the first key, then that in the new:—

ADDITIONAL EXERCISES

(WRITTEN WORK)

LESSON 39

Approach New Leading Tone From Above

Modulation by the Dominant Seventh Chord to the Dominant and the Subdominant Keys in Minor.

Modulation from a minor key to the minor key a perfect fifth higher is effected in essentially the same manner as from major to major. Take the new dominant seventh in any form as before but avoid making any voice move an augmented interval. In minor your best guide is this little rule:. Always go to the leading tone from above.

Ex. 51 (a) f I c V_7 ; (b) f I c V_3^4 ; (c) f I c V_2 ; (d) f I c V_2 Aug. 2nd Bad

The following models, one to the dominant key, the other to the subdominant, should be memorized, put on the blackboard in other keys, and played as before:—

Ex. 52 d I a V_2 I^6 IV I$_4^6$ V_7 I

Ex. 53 e I a V_7 I II$^{o6}_5$ I$_4^6$ V_7 I

HARMONY FOR EAR, EYE, AND KEYBOARD

A decided gain in the melodic line is obtained in Ex. 52 by resolving V^2 with an upward leap from the fifth of the chord. Compare with Ex. 29 (*b*).

EAR-TRAINING

Melodic:—

Moderato — Thomé, *Simple Confession (Simple Aveu)*

Andante maestoso — Wagner, *Pilgrims' Chorus from Tannhäuser*

Harmonic:—

I^5 IV^6_4 I $-^6$ V^6_4 I IV $-^6$ $-^8$ $-^6_4$ I

I V^6_5 I V $-^2$ I^6 IV I^6_4 $-$ V III^6 V_7 I

ASSIGNMENT

Keyboard Work: Modulate, using Ex. 52 as a model, from g–d, a–e, d–a, e–b, f–c.
    Modulate, using Ex. 53 as a model, from a–d, b–e, c–f, d–g, f♯–b.

---

[1] G in the tenor is really a passing tone between the fifth and the seventh of **V**, but forms a III^6 on the way.

Written Work: Harmonize and letter. Notice that the dashes in measure 6 continue the chord, though its position may change. The dash is always a sign of continuation of something already obtained:—

Note: The figures look forbidding at first glance, but they merely change our signature, thus suggesting the correct tones for the new key of g.

ADDITIONAL EXERCISES
(WRITTEN WORK)

American Guild of Organists, *Fellowship Ex Paper*

LESSON 40

Modulation by Dominant Seventh (Con.) From a Major Key to its Relative Minor and from a Minor Key to its Relative Major.

Ex. 54

(a) ... C I a V$_3^4$ I II^{o6} (b) Or begin this way C I a V$_3^4$ I

Ex. 55

(a) ... a I C V$_7$ I II$_5^6$ (b) Or begin this way a I C V$_5^6$ I

The above models have alternative beginnings. The cadences may be identical if desired. Still other beginnings can be made. Try them. In writing an original model, use care to preserve a fairly flexible melody. Do not permit yourself to write or play an original with an aimless soprano like the following:—

Inexcusably weak soprano

EAR-TRAINING

Key and Interval drill in minor.

Verbal Dictation in minor: One or two melodies which may afterwards be sung at sight.

Melodic: —

Guilmant, Sonata, N? 5

Beethoven, Sonata, Op 2, N? 3

German Folk-song

ASSIGNMENT

Keyboard Work: Modulate, using Ex. 54 as a model, from G–e, D–b, A–f♯, F–d, B♭–g.

Modulate, using Ex. 55 as a model, from each of the above minor keys to its relative major. In all these, select the beginning you prefer.

Written Work: Harmonize. In No. 2 the motive repetition justifies exact repetition of the harmony, thus strongly confirming the key of *a* minor. C major is therefore all the more welcome. To maintain the rising motive, the fifth in C V^7 is allowed to ascend, thus doubling the third in the new tonic triad. This is a clear case where it is better to break a general rule for the sake of the finer musical result:—

ADDITIONAL EXERCISES

(WRITTEN WORK)

LESSON 41

Common Chord Modulation In the folk-song and hymn tune every line of the poetry requires a cadence of some kind, and to avoid monotony some of the lines are often closed in related keys (keys that have many tones in common). The new key is not especially emphasized; and the original key is at once resumed by the succeeding line, if the melody permits. One or more of the chords. in a line which modulates, may be common to both keys. Call the last one of these common chords a "pivot-chord" and letter it in both keys as in the following models:—

Ex. 56

(a) C I { V / G I V$_{87}$ 1 }   C I IV vii°^{6} I   (b) C I vi III { vi^6 / G II^6 V } I

(c) C { C V^6 / G I^6 } G   (d) E♭ { E♭ I / B♭ IV } B♭ H$_3^4$ I$_4^2$ V$_7$ I

Keys Overlap The overlapping brackets (in Ex. 56) indicate how the keys may be thought of as interwoven; but while all of the chords in an entire line might be found in the key in which it ends, this is not assumed to be the case until some evidence of change of key appears. In Ex. 56 (*d*), the key of B♭ is considered in evidence with its II$_3^4$ chord followed by I$_4^6$. Consequently we say that the E♭ I is B♭ IV. Notice that if you think in the *so-fa* syllables, the last five notes of this line are *do, re, mi, re, do*. Apply this general principle of thinking entirely in your new key *from the moment its cadence emerges*.

Similar motion of all the voices and covered octaves, etc., from the end of a line (or cadence) to the first chord of the succeeding line, are not considered faulty.

SIGHT-SINGING AND EAR-TRAINING

Sight-Singing: Melodies which make a study of the rhythmic group ♪♪♪♪ and its various combinations

Melodic: Always tap each new rhythmic figure. In a melody such as the first, grasp the *pattern* at first hearing (a curve ⌒). Then focus the attention on the beginning tone of each repetition of this pattern (*mi so, do mi, la do, re mi*). It is then very easily memorized and written:—

ASSIGNMENT

Keyboard Work: Memorize Ex. 56 (a) and transpose it to several other keys. If this is easy for you, it will be well worth while to transpose the others in that set.

Written Work: Harmonize the following, taking care to determine the pivot chord and mark it in both keys. (The end of a line is here indicated by the ⌢, the first lines being very short.):—

LESSON 42

Common Chord Modulation (Con.) There is no new problem in this lesson except that your musicianship is challenged a bit in the written work. When you have a line that modulates, and there is no bass under it, you may need to try it in various ways. There may be more than one good solution. If you find two good settings of the same line so much the better.

SIGHT-SINGING AND EAR-TRAINING

Sight-Singing: Melodies which continue the study of rhythmic groups.

Harmonic:—

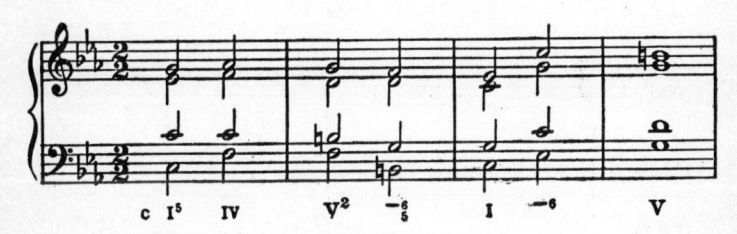

ASSIGNMENT

Keyboard Work: Transpose the following, beginning in c, d, e, and f :—

Written Work: Harmonize No. 1 as usual. In No. 2 the bass is given *unfigured*. This means that you are to figure it, selecting inversions that you consider suitable. You may need an accidental or two, but *never change a given part*. Your best fun will be with No. 3 :—

J. S. Bach

J. S. Bach

LESSON 43

Bach's Figured Chorals   When Johann Sebastian Bach was doing his great work in Leipzig as choir leader, organist, and composer, he placed figured basses under a large number of choral melodies, at the request of his brother-in-law in Vienna; and these were published at the time in a hymn book commonly referred to as Schemelli's Gesangbuch. In those days, the organist played the full harmony, as suggested by the figures, and the congregation all sang the choral melody. The figured choral in this lesson is from that interesting old book, from which seventy-five of Bach's chorals were later selected and printed for precisely the purpose which this one serves you.

Before beginning the Bach Choral, notice the significance of the dash after a figure *when the bass moves*, as at (*a*). A dash means continuation, hence the IV must be kept and the B in the bass treated as a passing tone. This is not at all like (*b*), where the second 6 means another chord. At (*c*), the dashes continue the chord while the bass A is an embellishment. Also note the parallel fifths in (*d*). The B, though but a passing tone, is here a trouble maker. For correction, double the third in the IV, as at (*a*):—

SIGHT-SINGING AND EAR-TRAINING

Sight-Reading: "Love's Old Sweet Song" — four parts as with previous folk-songs.

Melodic:

ASSIGNMENT

Keyboard Work: Like the organists in Bach's day, you may fill in, at sight, the figured choral lines in a previous lesson to be selected by the teacher.

Written Work: Harmonize the following Bach figured choral selected from the *Schemelli Gesangbuch*. Consider the second note of each pair of eighths as a passing note or embellishment not affecting the harmony:—

Arise, arise! the time is come
(Auf, auf! die rechte Zeit ist hier)

J. S. Bach

ADDITIONAL EXERCISES
(WRITTEN WORK)

My Heart is Broken
(Brich entzwei, mein armes Herze)

J. S. Bach

✢ Not a part of this chord but of the chord which follows — an *Anticipation*.

LESSON 44

Construction of a Hymn Tune In this lesson you are to compose a hymn tune by filling in the given framework (Ex. 57). This is adapted from a great melody in Händel's "Messiah." The choice of the cadences is worth your consideration, for in them lie the first principles of form, in music, in even the smallest work.

Importance of the Choice of Cadences The first cadence is imperfect in the tonic key. Händel does not leave the "home-key" or tonic, till he has said something worth while in it.

The second cadence brings us to a new level, the key a fifth higher. The first modulation is best to a key with one more sharp, and rather finer with a perfect cadence in the new key.

A half cadence in the tonic at the end of the third line leads toward home.

A perfect cadence in the tonic is reserved till the last. This cadence, however, is suited to the first line also, thus confirming the tonic.

The foregoing hints must be regarded as the merest suggestion of what lies behind a composer's procedure. You will find them apparently contradicted on every other page of any good hymn book, but, in their essence, they are true for all that.

While you are expected to make your original hymn tune fit these cadences, the choice of everything else is in your hands. Your vocabulary already includes repeated chords, passing tones, and all the harmony which is needed. It is not profitable, however, to try to "make up" a tune at the piano and write what you cannot analyze.

Framework of a Hymn Tune

Adapted from Händel

Ex. 57

A bound-less love He bore man-kind;
O may at least a part
Of that strong love des-cend, and find
A place in ev-ry heart.

SIGHT-SINGING AND EAR-TRAINING

Sight-Singing: Melodies involving ♩. ♪ . For the first few times that this rhythmic figure is sung, the teacher should play an accompaniment of ♬♬ so that the class may learn to sing the first tone (♪.) exactly three times as long as the second (♪) Carelessness leads to a substitution of ♩ ♪ (triplet) for ♩. ♪ . Any student having trouble with this rhythm should learn to skip !

Melodic:— ♪♫

Mendelssohn, *Elijah*

ASSIGNMENT

Keyboard Work: Review modulation by the dominant seventh chord.

Written Work: Compose a hymn tune by completing Ex. 57.

ADDITIONAL EXERCISES

(WRITTEN WORK)

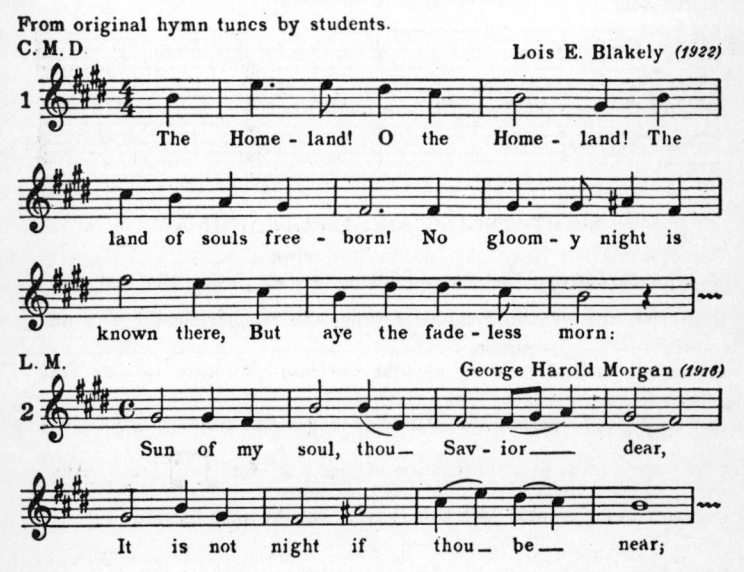

From original hymn tunes by students.

C. M. D.

Lois E. Blakely *(1922)*

1. The Home-land! O the Home-land! The land of souls free-born! No gloom-y night is known there, But aye the fade-less morn:

L. M.

George Harold Morgan *(1916)*

2. Sun of my soul, thou Sav-ior dear, It is not night if thou be near;

LESSON 45

Original Work In planning a piece of original composition in a small form like the hymn tune or folksong, you should lay out a tentative framework much like the one you completed in the last lesson. Write the stanza you have selected, scan each verse and place the bars of your measures where the accent of words and measure will coincide. This is highly important. Then you are ready to consider the kind of melody and harmony which you will use and to sketch in your plan of modulation, if you use any modulation.

As to the kind of tune you will write, the field is so vast that you may feel lost at first. It will help you here to consider three types and concentrate your effort on one of them.

Three Types Compared The *first type* is well illustrated in the music to Luther's great hymn, "A Mighty Fortress is Our God." This dates from the early sixteenth century and is as solidly built as the castle in which Luther himself was for a time imprisoned. No greater hymn was ever written, and the music is worthy its noble place; but nowadays we do not conceive our church tunes in this way. To hang a chord (and sometimes two of them) around the neck of each syllable and to finish most of the lines with a hold, was according to the best idiom of that day, but it would be strange if you preferred to write in that style now.

The *second type* is exemplified by Sullivan's noble music "Onward Christian Soldiers." This, with its swinging melody, chord repetition, and two harmonies to the bar (seldom more than two) embodies the optimism and freedom of more recent years. Its marchers move with no leaden feet. Other fine models of this type are so plentiful that you need but refer to any standard collection. This type is recommended and doubtless will appeal to you.

132 HARMONY FOR EAR, EYE, AND KEYBOARD

The *third type* is presented as a specimen of *what not to do*. A trivial melody hung on a poverty-stricken harmony, depends for its appeal entirely upon a cheap rhythm. If you will play the following chords, in the rhythm indicated just above them, you will know the type and avoid it. Here is a faithful picture of the exact harmony and rhythm of a well known "revival" tune:—

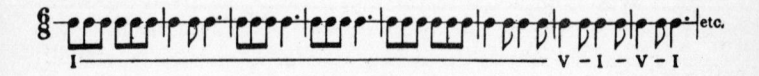

EAR-TRAINING

Two-part: —

Harmonic: —

Listen to this in a number of keys. Note the progression downward by thirds in the bass.

I^8 VI   IV   II   I$^6_4$ V$_7$ I

ASSIGNMENT

Keyboard Work: Continue work in modulation by the dominant seventh.

Written Work: Select the words of a fine hymn and bring it set to the best original music you can write. Let this model be *long meter*, which gives you eight syllables to the verse, with four verses in the stanza. These are indicated by "L. M." in the hymn book.

ADDITIONAL EXERCISES
(EAR-TRAINING REVIEW)

1. Schubert, *The Shepherd's Lament*

2. Mozart, *Sonata, No. 9*

3. Beethoven, *Sonata, Op. 14, No. 1*

4. Chopin, *Nocturne, Op. 55, No. 1*

5. Schubert, *Moment Musical, Op. 94, No. 3*

6. Schubert, *Who is Sylvia?*

7. Schubert, *Serenade*

LESSON 46

Next-Related Keys The *next-related keys* to any given key are those whose signatures do not differ from its signature by more than one sharp or flat. For any major key, the next-related keys are its dominant and subdominant major, and their three relative minors; and for any minor key, its dominant and subdominant minor, and their three relative majors. But a visual memory of all this is best, and is obtained from a glance at the following:—

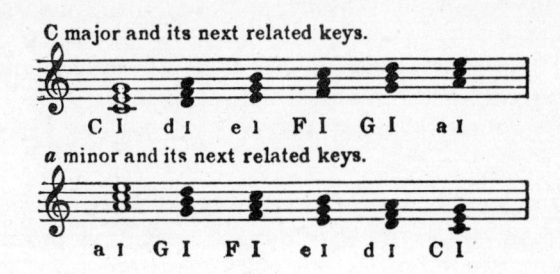

C major and its next related keys.

C I   d I   e I   F I   G I   a I

a minor and its next related keys.

a I   G I   F I   e I   d I   C I

Completing the Set of Modulations by V^7, to Next Related Keys To the modulations by the dominant seventh which you have already learned, we have but to add four others to complete the set of modulations by V^7 from any key to each of its next-related keys. From C there are **two** modulations as follows:—

Ex. 58

(a) C I   d V_7 I   IV   (b) C I^6 d V^4_3 I $II^{o\sharp}_5$

[Ex. musical notation with labels: C I eV₇ I I⁰⁶ ‖ C I eV₇ I IV]

In (c) and (d), *modulating a major third up*, we have a unique problem in modulation. It is precisely like the progression VI–V in minor; and we must here double the third in the first chord (the old tonic) to avoid an augmented second.

The remaining two modulations are from *a* minor, as follows (cadencing in any of the usual ways):—

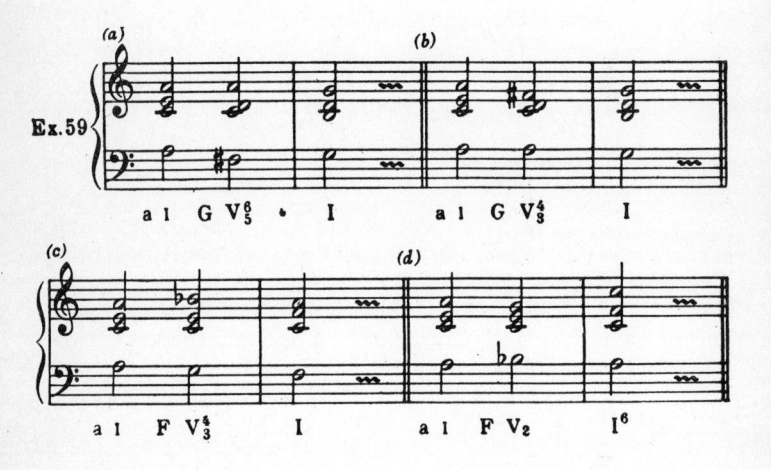

Ex. 59

(a) a 1 G V⁶₅ • I
(b) a 1 G V⁴₃ I
(c) a 1 F V⁴₃ I
(d) a 1 F V₂ I⁶

There are several other ways of approaching the new dominant seventh. These are offered as some of the smoothest. You are not expected to learn all these at once, but it will be fine to know them all by the time of the final review.

SIGHT-SINGING AND EAR-TRAINING

Sight-Singing: As soon as the book of sight-singing melodies has been completed, arrange to supply the class with some material to read at sight. If no additional books are available, copy melodies on the board from time to time.

Harmonic: Compare the sound of IV and II⁶ in the following models. Also listen to (*a*) and (*b*) with the third of the first chord in the soprano. Transpose these two positions to minor. Why not put the fifths in the soprano?

ASSIGNMENT

Keyboard Work: Modulate by the dominant seventh, using Ex. 58(*a*), or (*b*), as a model, from C–d, G–a, F–g, B♭–c, E–f♯.

Written Work: If your last piece was a success you will enjoy writing a processional or marching song. In *101 Best Songs* play over "March of the Men of Harlech," *Ward's* "O Mother Dear, Jerusalem," and *Mendelssohn's* "Hark! the Herald Angels Sing." Get fully into the spirit of these inspiring pieces, select words giving suitable scope (or the teacher will assign them), and bring "the best ever" next time. Plan a good variety in your cadences (not too much) and give your piece a fine swing. No matter if you flounder a bit and certain spots refuse to come out right, — bring the whole processional in pencil. Since the following lesson will be a review, time can be allowed for a finished ink-copy of your piece after the teacher has made necessary suggestions on the first draft.

LESSON 47

Ear-Training Review This review will emphasize the points which the teacher considers most important for the class concerned.

Keyboard Work Review *Modulation by the dominant seventh chord.*

To the dominant or subdominant:—
1. C–G   d–g   F–C   a–e   F–B♭
2. d–a   A–D   b–e   c–g   A–E
3. E♭–B♭   F♯–B   F–C   g–c   e–b

From a major or minor key to its relative:—
4. C–a   a–C   G–e   d–F   A♭–f
5. D–b   b–D   c♯–E   A–f♯   g–B♭
6. E–c♯   F–d   c–E♭   g♯–B   B♭–g

From a major key to the minor key a major second higher:—
7. C–d   G–a   B♭–c   F–g   A–b
8. E♭–f   D–e   E–f♯   D♭–e♭   A♭–b♭

Written Work Review A lesson should contain one number from each of the three groups.

Group 1

Modulation by the dominant seventh chord:—

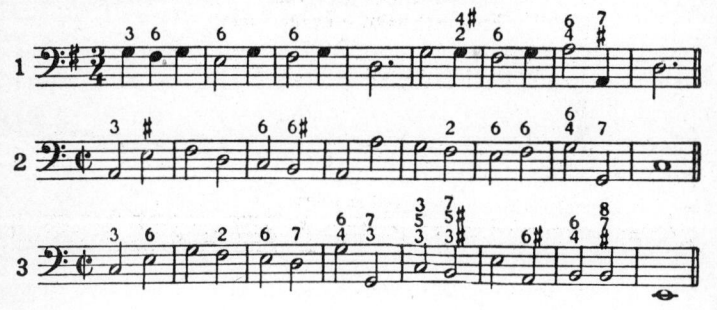

Group 2

Choral lines which modulate:—

Group 3

Chorals: Harmonize, figure the chords, and name the cadences:—

According to Thy mercy, Lord, deal Thou with me
(Mach's mit mir, Gott, nach deiner Güt')

Rejoice, my soul
(Freu' dich sehr, o meine Seele)

(Abridged ending)

HARMONY FOR EAR, EYE, AND KEYBOARD 139

Dearest Jesus, we are here
(Liebster Jesu, wir sind hier)

ADDITIONAL EXERCISES
(WRITTEN WORK)

New Courage take, my Weakened Spirit
(Ermuntre dich, mein schwacher Geist)

I love Jesus every hour
(Ich liebe Jesum alle Stund')

LESSON 48

The Suspension A *Suspension* is an *accented, prepared* dissonance which temporarily displaces the chord tone to which it resolves by going down a degree. It sometimes goes up (especially when prepared by the leading tone) and then it is called a *Retardation*. The suspension is indicated by (S) and the retardation by (R).

Ex. 60

Play Ex. 60 and analyze it, through both ear and eye. In (*a*) the suspension is a real dissonance. You can feel how it must resolve. In (*b*) the suspension is clearly not a part of the expected chord, therefore it sounds dissonant and wants to resolve as before. At (*c*) both these suspensions appear simultaneously. Here is a new way of looking at the six-four chord (the best way) and it will explain why we have been so careful in its use. While we can figure this chord I_4^6, as you see, it is really a V with two suspensions. At (*d*) these two suspensions must now appear in their true colors; for with the seventh in the tenor the six-four chord, in which they have been previously hidden, now disappears. At (*e*) the leading tone prepares a retardation in the soprano.

A detailed study of suspensions would be out of place here, but the above example will enable you to recognize them and to write them in the soprano or alto, or possibly in the tenor. Remember that the suspension, by its definition, first displaces a chord tone and then goes to it. Our pleasure in the suspension is not that it is dissonant, but that it delays briefly the entry of the chord tone and thus adds to the interest which the music awakens. Therefore you should not spoil the purpose of a suspension by letting some other voice sing this delayed tone simultaneously with the suspension. The bass, *at least a ninth lower* (possibly the tenor), is an exception to this *if it is not the third of a major chord.* This is quite enough for our present purpose.

EAR-TRAINING

[1] **Chord Color:** Use the following shorthand for this work:—

Major triad |	Augmented triad |'
Minor triad ı	Dominant seventh color, not
Diminished triad ı°	necessarily root position. V⁷

The teacher will play exercises similar to the following, for the class to indicate *chord color only*:—

Solution | ı° | | V₇ V₇ | | V₇ | ı' |

Harmonic: Exercises comparing the sound of IV and II⁶. (See models in Lesson 46.)

ASSIGNMENT

Keyboard Work: Transpose Ex. 60 to A, B, C, D, B♭, and G♭. Modulate by the dominant seventh, using Ex. 59(*a*), or (*b*), as a model, from a–G, e–D, c–B♭, f♯–E, g–F.

Written Work: Transpose the following model to B♭, number the chords, as usual, and indicate the suspensions and the retardation by the proper letters, as already begun:—

[1] From *Class Work in Music* by permission of Blanche Dingley Mathew.

142 HARMONY FOR EAR, EYE, AND KEYBOARD

[musical example 1, with figures: G I —6 V —6/5]

To show clearly the use of figures in figured bass requiring suspensions, the above exercise should be minutely analyzed in comparison with the following, which is its own bass, figured. This would make a valuable piece of board work in class also, not comparing with the model till you are through:—

[musical example 2]

ADDITIONAL EXERCISES
(WRITTEN WORK)

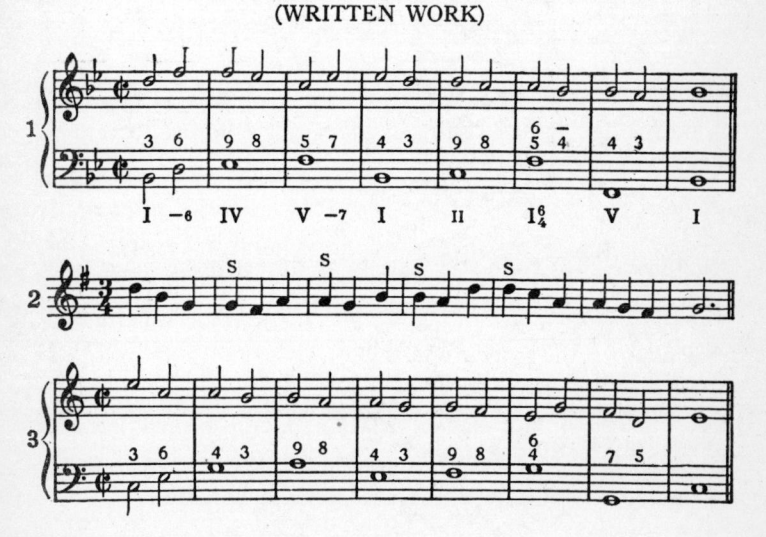

[musical example 1, with figures: I —6 IV V —7 I II I 6/4 V I]

[musical example 2]

[musical example 3]

LESSON 49

Harmonizing a Folk-Song as a Little Piece for the Piano

Facility in harmonizing a folk-song in the style of a little piano piece depends largely upon the ability to recognize the ornaments *for the purpose of looking past them* to the strong simple framework which the primary chords supply. These tunes abound in passing tones, embellishments, and suspensions, which lend grace and lightness to the melody, but which must be ignored when you choose the chords. *Don't harmonize your ornaments.*

Ex. 61

Play Ex. 61 and observe how it differs from the sturdy four-part harmony in a choral:

Here is a very simple chord foundation mostly one harmony to the measure in a light, dainty outline.

No harmony under the first weak beat.

Passing tones in both alto and soprano, and one in the bass, lend flexibility.

Suspensions also lend a charm and the melody is prettier with them. Play it without them and compare.

144 HARMONY FOR EAR, EYE, AND KEYBOARD

For a very young player you could write for the left hand just the plain bass notes, omitting the quarters which, while they make it fuller, yet add nothing to the harmony, as in Ex. 62 (*a*).

With a single line of melody, instead of the double thirds, you could play the chords in the left hand and get about the same effect (*b*).

EAR-TRAINING

Chord Color: Continue the work of last lesson.

Melodic: From this point on, the melodies may contain any of the rhythms we have studied. It is a good plan to sing the count, instead of the syllables, whenever one is in doubt about the rhythm. While singing, put in tiny numbers to indicate exactly where each beat comes. If several tones occur on one beat, determine whether they are equal or unequal in value.

ASSIGNMENT

Keyboard Work: Play the melody given below in the right hand with chords in the left to harmonize it, one chord only to each bar. Do not try to harmonize a suspension. Watch for the entry of the new key.

Written Work: Harmonize with a left hand part, as indicated. Label all the ornaments:—

Wanderer's Song
(Wanderlied)

Folk-song (1827)

ADDITIONAL EXERCISES
(WRITTEN WORK)

Folk-song (1815)

LESSON 50

The Appoggiatura An *unprepared* suspension is called an *Appoggiatura*. It is best on an accent but may be unaccented. It resolves by going down or up a degree to the chord tone it has displaced. When it goes up it likes to behave like a leading tone (resolving up a half step) and this often occasions the use of a chromatic tone. This in no way alters the key. The suspension can be considered, in a general way, as a dignified elder daughter in the family of ornaments — the appoggiatura is her gay young sister. Sign (Ap).

Broken Chord Accompaniment Broken chord accompaniment is a purely instrumental type of harmony. In it the individual voices lose their melodic significance, and consequently the rules for pure part writing are somewhat relaxed; but when reduced again to solid chords (always a good test), it should be evident that every reasonable attention has been paid to the principles of good chord connection. Before inventing some original accompaniments, the following examples should be clearly understood:—

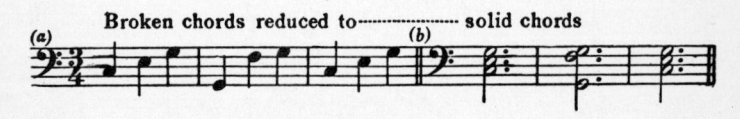

HARMONY FOR EAR, EYE, AND KEYBOARD   147

Overlapping, as in the (apparent) tenor and bass of Ex. 64(a), is written rather freely. In this case, after beginning as we do in the first measure, it is better to maintain the figure within the octave than to alter it or spread it out too much. A figure, once chosen, should be rather consistently maintained at least through several chords. To do this, one must not be too particular about doubling, overlapping, etc. But the chord figure generally omits the leading tone when this is supplied in the melody, as in (b). Your best guide in all these matters will be good models, from every one of which you can obtain ideas.

Ex. 64

SIGHT-SINGING AND EAR-TRAINING

Sight-Singing.

Harmonic:—

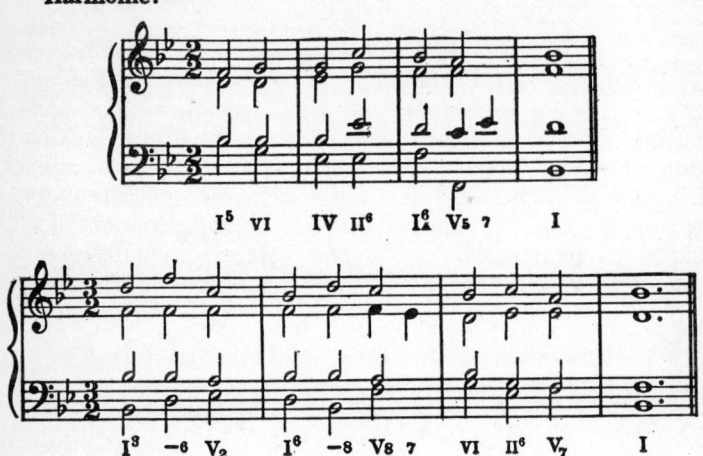

I^5 VI IV II^6 I$^6_4$ V$_5$ 7 I

I^3 —6 V$_2$ I^6 —8 V$_8$ 7 VI II^6 V$_7$ I

ASSIGNMENT

Keyboard Work: Modulate by the dominant seventh, using Ex. 59(*c*), or (*d*), as a model, from a–F, g–E♭, c–A♭, b–G, c♯–A, d♯–B.

Written Work: Harmonize the following tune with a broken chord accompaniment continued as begun. For contrast, you might use a different figure for the few measures where it is in the dominant key. With the return of the first theme, resume the original chord figure. Figure the chords, the change of key, and indicate the appoggiaturas and passing tones as before:—

LESSON 51

Construction of a Small Primary Form

The folk-song assigned in the last lesson, is a typical *Small Primary Form*. It is in B♭. Play the first four measures and notice their close in an imperfect authentic cadence; the next four and their ending with a perfect authentic cadence. This completes the first period. Now come four measures of contrast, in both key and material, closing with an authentic cadence in F. But the tonic in F is easily accepted as B♭ V, which leads naturally to a return of the original material in the tonic key, and a strong final cadence. This little plan is best seen when charted as follows:—

A Small Primary Form

16 measures				
4 meas.	4 meas.	4 meas. xxxxxxxx	4 meas.
Thesis	Antithesis	Thesis	Antithesis
First Period		Second Period	

This form will be very clear to you if you will fix in mind the cadence symbol used at the end of each four-measure line, associating it with the music as you play it over. Our model uses Nos. 1, 2, 4, and 6 in the following list:—

Cadence Symbols [1]

1. ─────< Half cadence in the tonic key.
2. ─────┤ Perfect authentic cadence in the tonic key.
3. ────── Imperfect authentic cadence in the tonic key.
4. ─────■ Authentic cadence in the dominant key.
5. ─────~ Authentic cadence in the mediant key.
6. xxxxxxxxxxx Contrasting material. (Not in itself a cadence.)

[1] These symbols are taken from Lehmann's *Form in Music* with permission of the publishers, A. G. Comings and Son.

Considerable variety is obtained in the choice of cadences without departing from this form, two other types of which are charted below. A coda is frequently added. This often improves the proportions but contains no new material; for, as the name indicates, a coda is a "tail," and could be removed without really altering the form.

Interpret the symbols in the following small primary forms:—

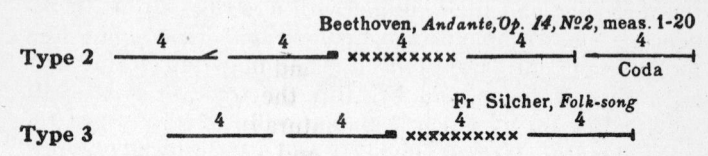

Type 2 — Beethoven, *Andante, Op. 14, No 2*, meas. 1-20 — 4 — 4 — xxxxxxxxx 4 — 4 — Coda

Type 3 — 4 — 4 — Fr Silcher, *Folk-song* xxxxxxxxx 4 — 4

The form of the celebrated "Minuet", by Beethoven, beginning

is like Type No. 3, with each period repeated. Repetition does not change the form. The *Trio* of this minuet is also in this form.

If available, all the pieces named should be played in class and studied by ear, as well as by the eye. Get a feeling of the proportion of one part to another, the variety afforded by the cadences, the unity in the repetition of certain motives, etc. It is good fun to try your hand at composing an original primary form, provided you lay out your plan intelligently.

EAR-TRAINING

Melodic: First use this phrase as ear-training. Then let the pupil use it as the first half of two or three periods. He will write out each antithesis and be ready to sing his completed melodies for the class.

HARMONY FOR EAR, EYE, AND KEYBOARD

Develop this motive into an eight-measure melody:—

ASSIGNMENT

Keyboard Work: Modulate by the dominant seventh, using Ex. 58(c), or (d), as a model, from C–e, B♭–d, G–b and A♭–c. Notice that this modulation is the only quite special one, *requiring a doubled third in the old tonic.*

Written Work: Write a small primary form which conforms in all its cadences to one of the three types charted in this lesson. Choose a type and adhere to it. Do not let your cadences run away with you.

ADDITIONAL EXERCISES

(WRITTEN WORK)

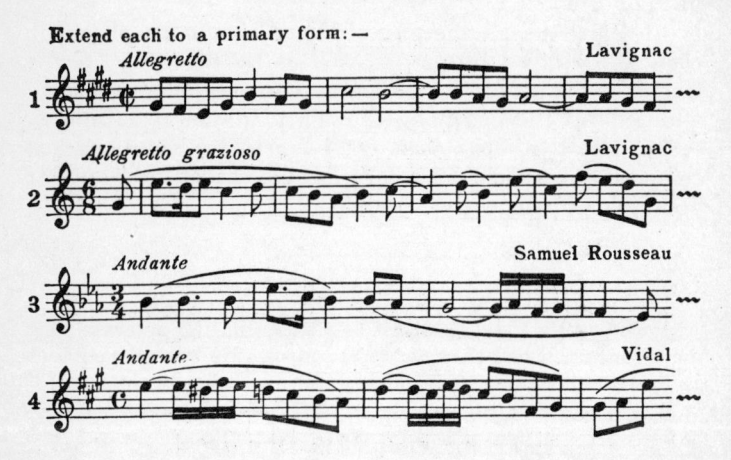

Extend each to a primary form:—

1. *Allegretto* — Lavignac
2. *Allegretto grazioso* — Lavignac
3. *Andante* — Samuel Rousseau
4. *Andante* — Vidal

LESSON 52

Choosing your Rhythms

Your original melodies are likely to be somewhat lacking in rhythmic interest if you do not observe what the masters have done in this line and work earnestly to catch their secret. We shall avoid discussion of the technical terms of composition and limit this lesson to a few hints on how to criticise your own efforts in the light of the following fine models from Beethoven, which will speak for themselves. We have bracketed each rhythmic unit. Some are one measure long, some two, some four. When a rhythm begins on a weak beat, its boundary is not the bar line. Play the examples several times. Use both ear and eye. Have you ever written a period in which your rhythms are so varied and so charmingly balanced?

HARMONY FOR EAR, EYE, AND KEYBOARD

Do not be troubled if your own efforts refuse to bring such beautiful results. Beethoven spent years on many of his melodies. To prove, too, that such a variety of rhythms is not a necessity, turn to Dvorak's well known "Humoreske," beginning:—

You may be relieved to discover what he did with *one rhythm four measures long* repeated *three* times. This piece is charming, but one of the most difficult things to do is to handle one rhythm only. And this is also a good thing to prove for yourself.

EAR-TRAINING

Harmonic: In this lesson, and the next, the teacher will play many short problems (3 or 4 chords each) for the class to analyze orally. These should include all of the progressions thus far studied. Use different positions, and both major and minor keys.

Suggestions:—

I V$_5^6$ I	I VI IV I
I IV$_4^6$ I	I V$_7$ VI
I I^6 V I	I II^6 V I
I V$_{82}$ I$_6$	I IV V$_3^4$ I

ASSIGNMENT

Keyboard Work: Begin a review of all the modulations by the dominant seventh chord. Think your new dominant seventh accurately and reach it *by the nearest road.* For next time try these: A–E, e–D, d–g, E–f♯, b–f♯, f–b♭, b–A, C♯–F♯.

Written Work: Write four eight-measure periods one of each of the following types. Do not harmonize them. If good enough they can be used later in primary forms. Do not let the suggestions regarding rhythm make you too self-conscious, or the music will wind up by not being written. Give your fancy free rein, and then check up your results by comparing your own rhythms, and their balance, with those quoted. It is better to imitate the models than to try to be too "original." Do not make a fetish of originality:—

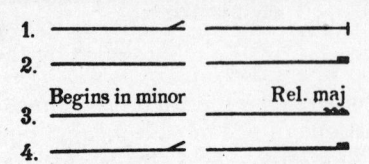

1. ⎯⎯⎯⎯⎯⎯⎯⎯⎯⎯⎯⎯⎯⎯
2. ⎯⎯⎯⎯⎯⎯⎯⎯⎯⎯⎯⎯⎯⎯
3. Begins in minor   Rel. maj
4. ⎯⎯⎯⎯⎯⎯⎯⎯⎯⎯⎯⎯⎯⎯

ADDITIONAL EXERCISES
(WRITTEN WORK)

Chapuis *(Paris)*

* To B instead of b, and a charming "side-trip" on the home journey. **Justified** here only because the bass is given..

LESSON 53

Ornamental Resolution   All the ornaments we have had (passing tones, appoggiatura, etc.) like to leap a third *to the other neighbor* of the chord tone which is their goal, before resolving. This is called *Ornamental Resolution* and affords the melody considerable additional freedom in melodic line without affecting the harmony. This is but one of a large family of ornamental resolutions, but will furnish all we need now. Focus your attention on the underlying principal chords and the ornaments will "shine out." Do not try to fit chords to them; they do not like it. The sign is "orna." preceded by the usual mark.

Violin with Piano Accompaniment   For next time, you are to complete the little piece begun for violin with piano accompaniment (Ex. 67). The melody has suspensions in it. The type of broken chord in this accompaniment is admirably adapted to these suspensions because the delayed tone need not be unpleasantly anticipated in the piano part, as for example in measure four. In measure two, the fifth of the chord in the piano is not strong enough to spoil the delayed fifth in the melody. In a piece of this type the melody may move in parallel octaves or unisons with any part of the accompaniment, but preferably not with the bass.

Summer Days

Ex 67 Moderato

EAR-TRAINING

Chord Color: Continue, as in Lessons 48 and 49.

Harmonic: Short review problems as in last lesson.

A good harmonization for *do ti la so* is I III IV I; and for *so la ti do*, I IV VII$^0_6$ I. Here is a good harmonization of the major scale. Play it and listen to it in all of the major keys:—

I^8-V I IV I^6 IV vii^0 I — III IV I^6 II^6 I$^6_4$ V$_7$ I

ASSIGNMENT

Keyboard Work: Continue review of modulation by the dominant seventh chord. The following list contains all the distances we have had (up per. 5; per 4; maj. 2; maj. 3; etc.) A–E, b–e, D–e, C–e, C–F, B♭–F, a–F, g–F, a–C, a♯–C♯, B–g♯.

Written Work: Bring *Summer Days* completed as a piece in small primary form, with a four-measure coda. If you, or a friend, can play the violin, your piece should be heard by the class.

ADDITIONAL EXERCISES

(WRITTEN WORK)

Tambourin

LESSON 54

Ear-Training Review   The character and difficulty of this review must be determined by the teacher.

Keyboard Work Review   Emphasis may well be laid upon modulation by the dominant seventh to every related key, and also upon harmonizing a folk-song at sight by playing the simple chords in the left hand, as in Lesson 49.

Written Work Review   A lesson should consist of the first three numbers or of the last number ("The Message of the Rose"). Also bring in, from your practical music, one illustration of each ornament studied thus far, and a small primary form.

Add the alto and tenor to No. 1. To Nos. 2 and 3 write a simple chord accompaniment for the left hand in the style of an easy piece for the piano:—

HARMONY FOR EAR, EYE, AND KEYBOARD 159

Harmonize No. 4 in the style indicated, one harmony only to each measure; mark the chords, keys, and ornaments; and make a chart of this little primary form, using the cadence symbols of Lesson 51:—

The Message of the Rose
(Der Rose Sendung)

F. H. Himmel (1814)

LESSON 55

The Dominant Ninth Chord

If we add another third to the dominant seventh chord (ninth from the root), there results the *Dominant Ninth Chord*. (See Ex. 68.) In major keys the ninth is major, a very mild dissonance, and introduced with considerable freedom; in minor the ninth is minor and harsh. In either mode the ninth resolves down a degree to the next chord. In five parts the fifth will be present and go up, for if it goes down the resulting parallel fifths are bad (*c*). In four parts the fifth is omitted (*d*). We shall here use the root position only, although two inversions (the first and third) are possible. The ninth must be kept a full ninth above the root and is best in the soprano. Figured $^9_7$.

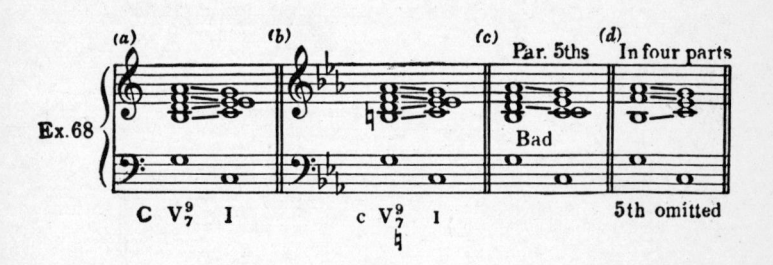

Like any chord member the ninth may leap (preferably down) to other tones of its own harmony, as in Ex. 69.

HARMONY FOR EAR, EYE, AND KEYBOARD

The Ninth as a Suspension or an Appoggiatura

A prepared ninth which resolves down to its own root, *before the chord changes*, is a suspension (not restricted to the soprano) and, in figured bass, is indicated by 9 8 or $\frac{9}{7}\frac{8}{-}$, depending on whether the chord is a triad or a seventh chord, as in Ex. 70 (*a*), (*b*). An unprepared ninth, as at (*c*) or (*d*), is clearly an appoggiatura.

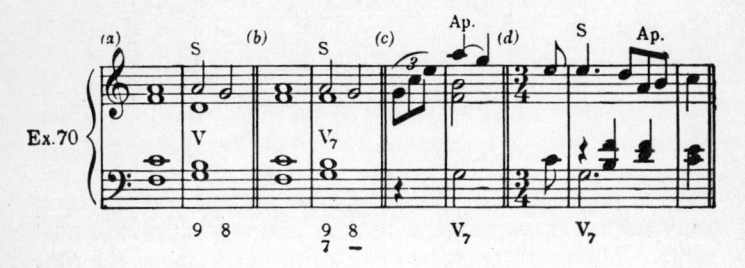

Ex. 70

SIGHT-SINGING AND EAR-TRAINING

Sight-Singing.

Harmonic: Modulation to closely related keys:—

The teacher will play simple modulations, on the order of the above model, to the dominant, subdominant, and relative major or minor key. The modulation may be made by the root position or an inversion of V⁷.

The class should follow closely the bass part. In the above model, the bass is *do ti la*, *la* becoming the new tonic. V$\frac{4}{3}$ is the only position of V⁷ resolving one degree downward to a root position of the tonic chord. Therefore this is a modulation down a minor third by V$\frac{4}{3}$. Any of these modulations may be reasoned out in a similar way.

162 HARMONY FOR EAR, EYE, AND KEYBOARD

ASSIGNMENT

Keyboard Work: Transpose Ex. 68(*d*) and 69 to other major keys.

Written Work: Harmonize and figure as usual:—

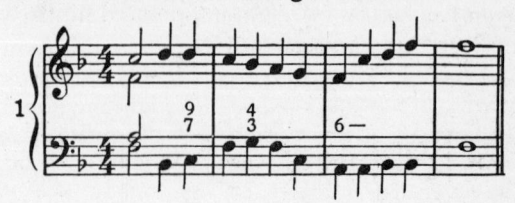

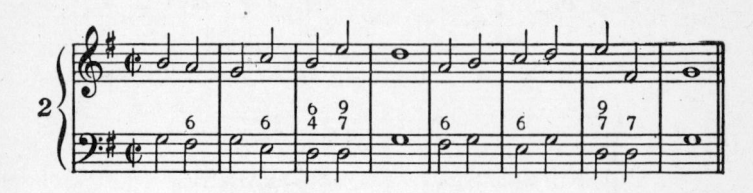

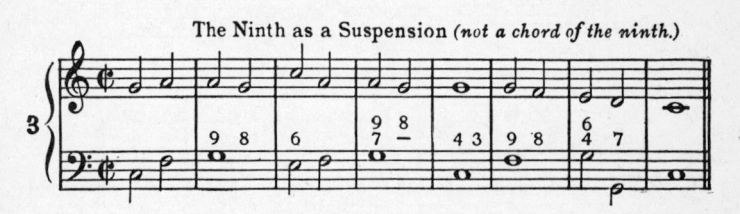

ADDITIONAL EXERCISES
(WRITTEN WORK)

LESSON 56

The Remaining Chords of the Seventh

We should now make a brief survey of the remaining chords of the seventh. There are two whose origin is the dominant ninth with the root omitted. Their resolution is precisely what it is when the original root (the dominant) is present. Because of their origin they are primary sevenths and do not require preparation. For simplicity, they are figured as seventh chords:—

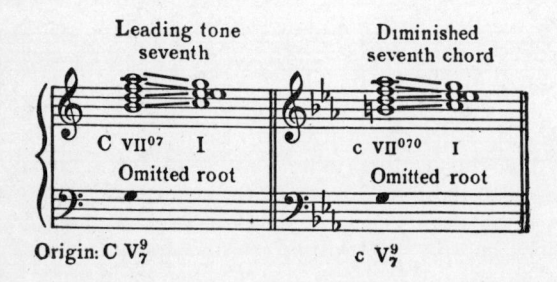

Leading tone seventh

C VII^{07} I
Omitted root

Origin: C V$^9_7$

Diminished seventh chord

c VII^{070} I
Omitted root

c V$^9_7$

The remaining secondary sevenths are as follows:—

C I$_7$,   III$_7$,   IV$_7$,   VI$_7$ c I$_7$,   III$'_7$,   IV,   VI$_7$

The seventh of all these secondary seventh chords must be prepared, and resolved down a degree. (Major sevenths that function like a leading tone and go up will not appear in our exercises.) In minor these sevenths are practically useless for us, but, in major, progressions like the following have a value, as we shall see, in certain kinds of composition where frequent resolution to chords of repose is purposely avoided. [See Ex. 71(a), (b).]

Ex. 71

(a) I II² V⁶₅ I⁶₃ IV⁶₅ VII⁰² III⁶₅ VI² II⁶₅ V I

(b) 7 7 7 7 7 7 7 7

Note that these are all cadencing resolutions, that in inversions every chord is complete, but that in root positions every other seventh chord omits its fifth. Also observe that the leading tone, instead of taking its normal resolution to the tonic, observes the sequence and does what its neighbors do.

These chords, in addition to the foregoing cadencing resolution, may progress to any chord which permits proper resolution of the seventh, as, for example, in Ex. 72 (a), and including passive resolution (b). In all of them the seventh may enter as a passing seventh (c).

Ex. 72

(a) I V I₇ VI⁶₅ IV⁴₃ II² VII⁰₇ V⁶₅ I (b) 7 6 (c) 6 ⁶₅ 8 7

EAR-TRAINING

Harmonic: Further drill on modulation by V^7, as illustrated in the last lesson.

HARMONY FOR EAR, EYE, AND KEYBOARD

From now on it will be well to review the weakest points in the year's work. No definite ear-training outline will be given, but it is assumed that the usual amount of time will be spent on aural work, selected at the teacher's discretion.

ASSIGNMENT

Keyboard Work: Transpose Ex. 71 (*a*) and (*b*), and Ex. 72 (*a*) to several other major keys.

Written Work: Harmonize:—

ADDITIONAL EXERCISES
(WRITTEN WORK)

Richter

Jadassohn

Tchaikovsky

Double Chant   Prout

LESSON 57

The Supertonic Seventh Chord Chromatically Altered
The supertonic seventh chord appears rather frequently with its third chromatically raised. This makes it precisely like the dominant seventh of the dominant key, and produces a modulation if desired; or it may continue in the tonic key, progressing the same as if it had not been altered. See Ex. 73 (a) and (b).

Ex. 73

C I   II^2 V^6 II^2 V$^6_5$ II$^6_5$
      [3♯]   [3♯]   [5♭]

In the above example at (a) the modulation, if considered at all, is transient; but this could be marked G V^2-I^6, if desired. At (b) the F♯ goes to F♮ directly, and the only explanation is that the key is C and that the F♯ is a chromatic alteration. This alteration is indicated in [ ].

The supertonic seventh chord also delights in other chromatic alterations, one of these being the lowered fifth, as at (c) above.

We have already seen that keys may follow each other closely, if desired, omitting any formal closing cadences. And now we come to an interesting application of the material in this and the preceding lesson, in constructing a prelude.

Construction of a Little Prelude
This type of piece is quite the opposite of a choral, or a folk-song, with their constantly recurring cadences. It is intended, rather, to be such a succession of chords as will admit no repose, to

speak of, till the end. As Bach uses it in many cases, it is a happily invented cadence formula enlivened with some broken chord figure which whisks you through a little "round trip" over the keyboard to get you ready for the fugue, or other piece, which may follow. Whether modulation occurs or not, there is no other feeling than one of pressing on *to the one final cadence* in the tonic. Here is a simplified example from Bach's first prelude in the *Well Tempered Clavichord*.

In the foregoing plan, the underlying principles of good form are carefully observed. There is enough in the tonic key to establish it first of all. The first modulation is to the dominant, toward the sharp side of the key, aggressive and forward looking. The place of contrast in a primary form, is here occupied by an inflection to keys on the flat side; i. e., to d minor and F major, thus giving balance to the tonality as a whole. Full closes are absolutely shunned. The final dominant chord is expanded to four measures one of which appears as a tonic six-four. In the third measure from the last, the alto clings to C, thus making it a suspension. The hold (⌢) you may interpret as three measures of tonic, if you like, and give the end some clever upward turn in broken chords, or a scale passage, ending perhaps on high C.

ASSIGNMENT

Keyboard Work: Play Ex. 73 (*a*), (*b*), (*c*), adding a suitable cadence in C to each one. Do the same with them in other major keys.

Written Work: Complete the *Prelude Plan*, Ex. 74, in the style in which it is begun, and figure the chords and keys as usual. If you consider a chord chromatically altered, but remaining in the tonic key, indicate the alteration in brackets, as shown in Ex. 73.

LESSON 58

Transient Modulation The value of transient modulation is beautifully shown by Beethoven in the little primary form, Type No. 2 (see Lesson 51), where the four measures of contrast consist of the following vigorous passage:—

Ex 75

C I^6 V$^4_3$ I F V^2 I^6 V$^4_3$ I

— d V$^4_3$ I VII$^0_8$ I^6 G VII$^0_7$ I C V—^{2} I^6
[7♭]

Notice the manner in which Beethoven reaches the key of G in the last full measure. This leading tone seventh has its seventh flat. This particular chromatic alteration is frequent and produces a diminished seventh which is identical with the corresponding chord in minor (Lesson 56). If desired, one can, at any time, thus substitute the diminished seventh chord for the dominant seventh.

One other point of interest in the above model: notice the suspension where G major is entered and the pleasing relief it affords after so many chords of equal length. If your modulations are well made and a suspension occasionally begs admission, give it a trial.

Modulating Sequences

A modulating sequence, like Ex. 76, extended until the original key is reached again, forms a valuable drill in both keyboard and written work. We say "drill" advisedly. Such a passage has no musical value; but, like scale practice, concentrates everything, for the time, in the one problem. It would be well for you, working in groups of two or three, to complete this sequence at the board. When you reach G♭, write it as F♯ and continue till you return to C.

A Sequence Modulating up a Perfect Fourth.

Ex. 76

C I⁶ F V$_5^6$ I B♭ V² I⁶ E♭ V$_5^6$ I A♭ V²

A passage like Ex. 77 has more musical value than an example like 76. The sequence design is longer. The fourth measure leads to G I in the proper position to begin the new design, that is, with the root in the soprano, as at first. To repeat this design you must select your keys, both as to mode and distance, exactly as in these first four measures — another good blackboard problem. This will keep moving down, but since it is merely an exercise, begin the new design an octave higher at pleasure:—

Ex. 77

C I a V$_3^4$ I d V² I⁶ G V$_5^6$ I V₇ I e V$_3^4$

HARMONY FOR EAR, EYE, AND KEYBOARD 171

ASSIGNMENT

Keyboard Work: Play Ex. 76 and continue it till you reach C again. Transpose the design of Ex. 77, beginning in D, in B♭ and in F. The next is harder to do and optional; i. e., to continue the sequence (Ex. 77) till you reach B.

Written Work: Harmonize the following two types of exercise. In the first one, the 4 3 at the end is the figured bass sign for the third suspended in the V⁷ chord. In the second one, reach each new tonic, as indicated, through some form of its dominant seventh chord. Except at the end, this is *unfigured;* therefore you must use inversions, sharps, etc., as needed. In both exercises there appears in the cadence the supertonic seventh chord with flatted fifth.

ADDITIONAL EXERCISES
(WRITTEN WORK)

LESSON 59

Pianoforte Style Chiefly Homophonic
In polyphonic music all the voices are considered equal in melodic importance. In homophonic music there is a chief melody to which the other parts are subordinate. These subordinate parts are many or few in number, they are used as broken or repeated chords, or at times they may imitate the chief melody. Again, the composer may give the subordinate parts important roles and, in so far as they become of equal importance with the chief melody, the music becomes polyphonic again. But, beginning with Beethoven, most pianoforte music is homophonic. When you harmonize a folk-song with simple chords, as in previous lessons, you are writing the simplest homophonic music. A more artistic treatment of a melody is seen in the "Nocturne" from the *Midsummer Night's Dream* music. Mendelssohn's mastery of part-writing is shown even here. You can see his harmonization of the first few measures, for these are a faithful copy of his own pianoforte score as reduced from the original for orchestra. It is not a question here of real four-part writing, as in the choral. There may be momentarily but two tones sounding together; and again there may be three, four, five, or six. The effect of the whole is that of an enchanting melody floating on broad simple chords. Notice how Mendelssohn's supporting harmony gains in refinement through its approach to the style of real voices, yet refuses to sacrifice a certain pianistic freedom. To finish this in the style in which it is begun will test your musicianship. If you have studied this music and happen to know it well, so much the better; but in that case you may prefer to try your hand at an original piece in the same vein instead of harmonizing this melody.

ASSIGNMENT

Keyboard Work: Review, as determined by the teacher.

HARMONY FOR EAR, EYE, AND KEYBOARD

Written Work: Complete the "Nocturne" in the style of Mendelssohn.

Nocturne

Mendelssohn, *Midsummer Night's Dream*

LESSON 60

With the following well known melody we close the studies in this little book. The melody of the "Soldiers' Chorus" swings exultantly along over a simple chord accompaniment — a style with which you are already familiar. Notice the form of this piece, with its fine contrast beginning in G (measure 9) and the stirring return, at the Da Capo, to the first theme.

ASSIGNMENT

Keyboard Work: To be determined by the teacher, as in Lesson 59.

Written Work: Complete the March in the style in which it is begun. If you have shown talent for composition, your teacher will doubtless prefer to have you write an *original March in this form* and allow you extra time in which to perfect it and to make a beautiful copy on full size music paper. Such a piece of music would be suitable for various festive occasions. Moreover, if arranged for the school orchestra or band and played well, it might be a delightful revelation of what a first year harmony student can accomplish.

March
Soldiers' Chorus

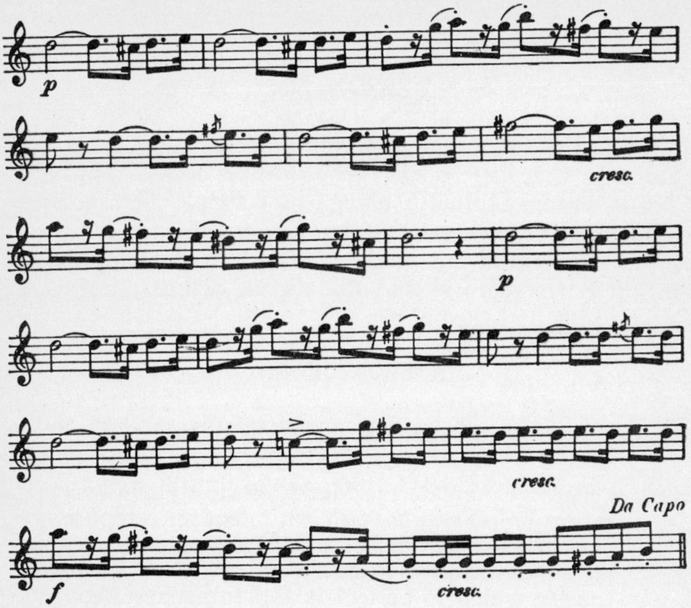
p
cresc.
p
cresc.
Da Capo
f
cresc.

APPENDIX A

Reference List

I. SIGHT-SINGING AND VERBAL DICTATION:

    Beach, *Easy Melodies for Sight-Singing.*
    Cole and Lewis, *Melodia* (Bks. I, II). Particularly good for two-part work.
    Cole, *Musical Dictation.*
    Dann, *Music Course* (*Third, Fourth and Fifth Readers*). The *Fourth Reader* contains some good minor melodies and some fine eye-training studies.
    Lavignac, *Solfège des solfèges* (Vol. 1A, 2A.)
    Lemoine and Carulli, *Seventy-two Solfeggi for Two Voices.*
    Natural Music Course (*Melodic Third Reader*). Contains some good minor material for Verbal Dictation.
    New Educational Music Course (*First Reader and Intermediate Song Reader*). The latter is divided into parts which take up, in turn, intervals, rhythm, chromatics, and three-part work.
    Progressive Music Series (Bks. I, II, III). Some good material in minor keys in Bk. III.

II. FOLK-SONGS:

    Bantock, *One Hundred Folk-songs of all Nations.*
    Whitehead, *Folk-songs and other songs for Children.*
    Twice 55 Community Songs.
    Liberty Chorus Song Book.
    101 *Best Songs.*

III. MELODIES FOR DICTATION:

    Alchin, *Ear Training for Teacher and Pupil.*
    Alchin, *Tone Thinking and Ear Training.* All grades of material.
    Codas (Nos. 166-172).
    Congdon, *Music Readers* (Bks. I, II, III). Very simple material.
    Dann, *Manual to Music Course.* All grades of material.

Diller, *First Theory Book*.
Farnsworth and Kraft, *Tonal Phrase Book* (Bks. II, III).
Heacox, *Ear-Training*. Good collection of famous themes.
Shinn, *Melodic Ear Training* (Bk. I). Advanced material.
Wedge, *Ear-Training and Sight-Singing*. All grades of material.

IV. HARMONIC DICTATION:

Heacox, *Keyboard-Training in Harmony* (Parts I, II). Contains a fund of additional exercises for both ear and keyboard work.
Robinson, *Aural Harmony* (Part I).

V. NOTATION:

Gehrkens, *Music Notation and Terminology*.
Williams, *Story of Notation*.

VI. ADDITIONAL MATERIAL (for the harmony teacher and advanced student only):

Arensky, 1000 *Exercises*. Melodies and figured and unfigured basses. P. Jurgenson, Moscow, Russia.
Bach, *Geistliche Lieder und Arien aus Schemelli's Gesangbuch*, Breitkopf & Haertel, Leipzig.
Chapuis, *Leçons d' Harmonie*, Durand et fils, Paris.
Lavignac, *Leçons d' Harmonie* (1er, 2e, et 3e Recueil), Lemoine et Cie, Paris.

VII. RELATIVELY NEW TEXT-BOOKS (for the teacher's own library):

Hull, *Modern Harmony*.
Kitson, *The Evolution of Harmony*.
Lenormand, *A Study of Modern Harmony*.
Cutter, *Harmonic Analysis*.
Corder, *Modern Musical Composition*.
Stanford, *Musical Composition*.
Goetschius, *Lessons in Music Form*.
Lehmann, *The Analysis of Musical Form*.
Macpherson, *Form in Music* (chaps. I to XI.)

VIII. A FEW OF THE WIDELY USED STANDARD TEXTS:
Chadwick, *Harmony.*
Foote and Spalding, *Modern Harmony.*
Jadassohn, *Manual of Harmony.*
Goetschius, *The Theory and Practice of Tone-Relations.*
Prout, *Harmony.*
Richter, *Manual of Harmony.*
York, *Harmony Simplified.*

APPENDIX B

Suggested Examination Papers

When preparing examination papers in harmony the teacher should give careful attention to the following principles:

Range of the Questions — From a tentative list of all the points that have been presented in the course select a representative set and prepare the questions with these points strictly in view. Exclude points that have not been amply brought out in the daily work.

Difficulty — Temper the difficulty of each point according to the emphasis that has been laid upon it in the course. Avoid anything like a "catch question." Avoid, also, setting a question that unnecessarily repeats a point.

Length — The length will vary in the different schools according to the age of the pupils. Young pupils should not be given long examinations. The following papers are based upon the material in this book and are prepared for Juniors and Seniors in high school or for Freshmen in college—students for whom a 1½ to 2-hour examination is not excessive.

Grading — Methods of grading must vary according to the character of the paper. In a paper involving numerous details, as in the present instance, it is well to check over each answer on a basis of points. It is not till after all the papers have been thus examined by the teacher that he is ready to grade them.

Keyboard Work — Examination in keyboard work must, of course, be individual. The pupils should present themselves in turn, each being allowed four to five minutes. If the class is large a typed list of those who are to be examined may be posted at a convenient place outside the room. Those who are to play are thus saved a long wait, since it is understood that about fifteen pupils per hour will be called in turn into the room.

Ear-Training — The ear-training examination can be dictated to a whole class at the same time, several sections meeting together, if desired. The teacher will state the key, then sound the tonic chord, after which he will play the question twice, clearly, give the students ample time to write the solution without feeling hurried (two or three minutes), then play once more for a final hearing. In the harmonic questions the student is expected to write the soprano, bass, and chord numerals. The three questions should require about twenty minutes.

Sight-Singing If it is desired to give final examinations in sight-singing, select new material, that this examination may be really a *sight* test. A typical test consists of two melodies, one involving tonal, the other, rhythmic problems. The procedure should be the same as for the keyboard examination, with three to four-minute individual appointments.

Here follow (pp. 181-4) four typical examination papers expressly prepared to cover the work in this book. Attention is called to the division of the lessons into four groups as indicated at the head of the papers. While it is not desired to dictate to experienced teachers, the divisions here suggested are recommended.

HARMONY FOR EAR, EYE, AND KEYBOARD 181

No. 1 — FINAL EXAMINATIONS — Lessons 1 to 19
Ear-Training

Points

(*10*) 1. Tonal: —

(*10*) 2. Melodic: —

(*10*) 3. Write the names of the following intervals —

Keyboard Work

(*5*) 4. Play and spell: Scale of A major, g minor original form, b minor harmonic form; major triads on B and A♭ changing each to minor.

(*5*) 5. Play: D I³-IV-I, G I⁸-V-I, B I⁵-IV-V-I, F I³-IV-I⁶₄-V-I.

(*10*) 6. Harmonize: —

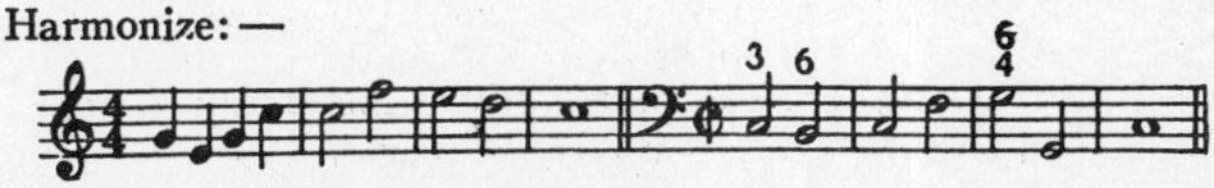

Written Work

(*5*) 7. Define: *Keynote, Dissonance, Cadence, Six-four Chord, Leading Tone.*

(*10*) 8. (a) Write the following scales and place the signature after each one: A♭, e orig. form, d♯ har. form.
    (b) Write: —

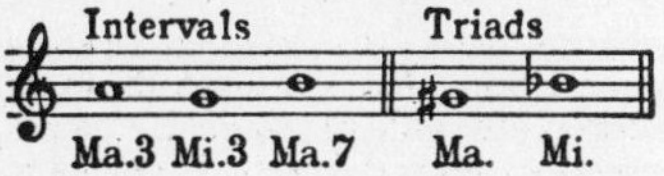

    Intervals   Triads
    Ma.3 Mi.3 Ma.7   Ma. Mi.

(*15*) 9. Supply soprano, alto, and tenor to the following figured bass, copy the figures, and supply the chord numerals: —

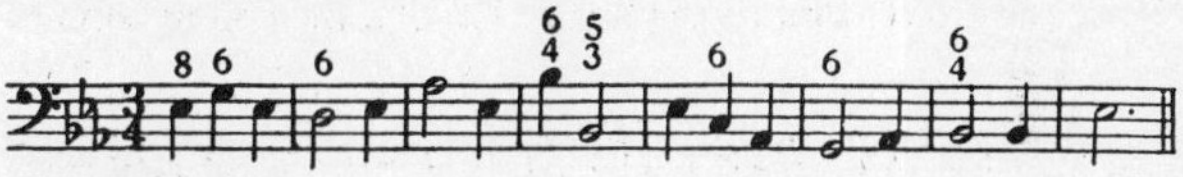

(*20*) 10. Harmonize the following soprano with primary triads. Use a few chords of the sixth, and two properly placed six-four chords. Figure fully: —

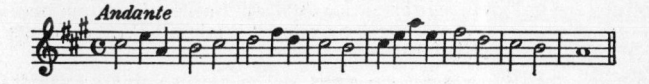

Andante

HARMONY FOR EAR, EYE, AND KEYBOARD

No. 2 — FINAL EXAMINATIONS — Lessons 20 to 37

Ear-Training

Points

(10) 1. Harmonic: —

(10) 2. Melodic: —

(10) 3. Two-part: —

Keyboard Work

(5) 4. Play, spell, and classify:
   (a) The three used kinds of *seconds, thirds,* and *fourths,* reckoned from F upward.
   (b) The scale of triads in d minor (har. form).

(5) 5. Play: F V$_3^4$-I, g I-II$_5^{06}$-V-I, E♭ I-II^6-I$_4^6$-V^7-I.

(10) 6. Harmonize this melody using all three inversions of V^7. Harmonize the bass so as to illustrate two special progressions in the minor keys: —

Written Work

(5) 7. Write the rules for: (a) Regular resolution of the Dominant Seventh Chord, (b) V-VI in minor, (c) II-V in any key.

(10) 8. Write the complete table of triads, i. e., a major, minor, diminished, and augmented triad with B as the root of each, and locate each in all the keys in which it can be found.

(15) 9. Supply soprano, alto, and tenor to this figured bass, copy the figures and supply the chord numerals. Give especial attention to the formation of a melodious soprano: —

(20) 10. Harmonize this melody as the Thesis of a Period. Write in four part harmony, using one or (at most) two chords to the measure. Figure the chords and label the passing tones and embellishments. Add an Antithesis of four measures that will close with a Perfect Plagal Cadence, harmonize and mark as before: —

No. 3 — FINAL EXAMINATIONS — Lessons 38 to 48

Ear-Training

Points

(10) 1. Melodic —

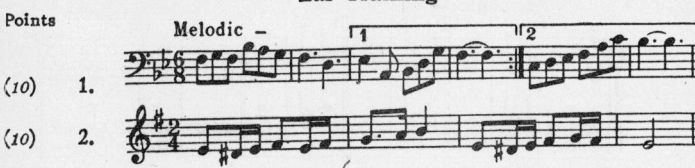

(10) 2.

(10) 3.

Keyboard Work

(5) 4. Modulate by the dominant seventh chord, adding a closing cadence: G to e, g to d.

(5) 5. Play: aI^8-G V^8-I, d I^5-g V^2-I^6-II^{o6}_5-V^{87}-I.

(10) 6. Harmonize. In the melody show a modulation by common chords, in the bass show two suspensions: —

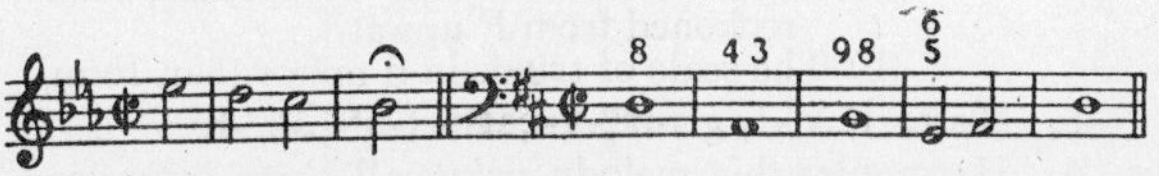

Written Work

(5) 7. Define: *Modulation, Closing Cadence*, as applied to a modulation, *Suspension*.

(10) 8. What are the *next related keys* to the key of e minor? In four-part harmony connect, in turn, the tonic triad of d minor with some inversion of the V^7 of each of its next-related keys (two chords only in each illustration).

(15) 9. Supply the alto and tenor, copy the figures, add chord numerals and key letters: —

(20) 10. Harmonize the following choral in four-part harmony. Figure fully. A few well placed suspensions will add to the value of your solution: —

No. 4 — FINAL EXAMINATIONS — Lessons 49 to 60
Ear-Training

Points

(10) 1. Melodic: —

(10) 2.

(10) 3. Harmonic: —

Keyboard Work

(5) 4. Modulate by the dominant seventh chord, adding a closing cadence: A to E, F to a, F♯ to g♯.

(5) 5. Play: C I-II$_5^6$ V I, E I-II^2-V$_5^6$-I.
        (5♭)   (3♯)

(10) 6. Harmonize the eight measures of a folk-song given below in question No. 10, with one chord to the measure in the left hand. Before beginning to play study the melody in order to plan your choice of chords.

Written Work

(5) 7. Write a short paragraph on the difference between homophonic music and polyphonic music.

(10) 8. In harmonizing a folk-song for the piano how should one plan the harmony? What must be done about passing tones, etc.? Using the cadence symbols, chart a typical folk-song that contains five four-measure phrases, a modulation, and contrast at a suitable place.

(15) 9. Unfigured bass. Supply the soprano, alto, and tenor. Where indicated reach a new tonic through its dominant seventh chord, and use a chromatically altered supertonic seventh chord in the cadence. Supply key letters, figuring, and chord numerals: —

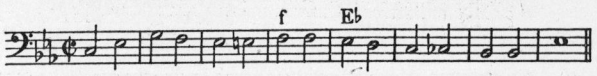

(20) 10. Extend the following melody to twenty measures thus completing a Small Primary Form. Do not harmonize but indicate the cadence you propose at the end of each phrase. Invent an accompaniment figure for the first two measures:—

Index

(The numbers refer to pages.)

Antithesis	41
Appoggiatura	146
Augmented second	37
Augmented fourth	112
Augmented triad	81
Bach figured chorals	125
Broken Chord accomp.	146
Broken Chord versions of a Period	66
Cadence, authentic, plagal, half	41
Cadence, deceptive	71
Cadence closing a modulation	167
Cadence symbols	149
Cadencing resolutions	102
Choice of cadences important	128
Chord repetition	24
Chord of Sixth	48, 52
—in succession	96
Chromatic scale	67
" alteration of supertonic seventh chord	166
Consonance	4
Construction of a hymn tune	128
" of a small primary form	149
" of a little prelude	166
Diatonic scale	3
Diminished seventh chord	163
" triad	81
Dissonance of the seventh in V^7	74
Dominant of the key	32
Dominant seventh chord, resolution, fifth omitted, importance of, introduction of seventh	74
Dominant seventh inversions	78
Dominant ninth chord	160
Doubling the root	7
—the third	59
—the fifth	59
—the leading tone, prohibited	100
Embellishment	61
Exceptions	99
Fifths, covered	87
—omitted in triad	59
—omitted in Dom. seventh	75
—parallel	16
Figured bass, sources, present use	46
Harmonizing 1-2 of scale	27
—a folk-song for piano	143
Hymn tune	
—construction of	128
—three types of	131
Intervals	29
Inversion of intervals	30
" of triads	48
Leading tone	32
—in IV^6-V^6	100
—approach to	114
—seventh chord	163
Licenses in sequence	105
Major scale	5
Mediant	32
Minor scales	35, 36
Modulation by dominant seventh	110, 114, 117, 130
Modulation by common chords	129
Modulation, transient	160
Modulatory sequence	174
Next related keys	131
Ninth as a suspension	162
Notation	27
Octaves, covered	84
—parallel	16
Original work	51, 69, 131, 149, 154, 157
Overlapping of voices	94
—of keys	120
Passing tones, unaccented	58
—accented	61
Period	41
Position	5
Position, close, open	12
Primary triads	6
—in minor	35
Relative keys	35
Resolution, of seventh	75, 102
—dominant ninth	160
—of suspension	140
—ornamental	155
Retardation	140
Rhythm, choosing	152
Rules	
For harmonizing a melody	15
for II-V	86
for II-I 6/4	90
for V-VI or VI-V in minor	93
Scales	
Major	5
Minor	35, 36
Chromatic	3
Secondary triads	86, 90, 93
Sequence	105
Similar motion of all parts	99
Six-four chord	48, 50
—in cadence	50
—embellishing	63
—ornamenting plagal cad.	63
—passing	63
Special names of members of keys	32
Supertonic triad	90
Supertonic seventh chord	102
—chromatically altered	166
Suspension	140
Seventh chords	163
Tendency of dim. and aug. intervals	73
Tendency of leading tone	33
—of the seventh of a chord	74
Thesis	41
Triads	
—table in major	82
—table in minor	84
—complete	84
Violin with piano accomp.	66